Blindnes[s]
Psycholo[gy]
Development in
Young Children

Edited by

Vicky Lewis and Glyn M. Collis

BPS
BOOKS Published by BPS Books
(The British Psychological Society)

First published in 1997 by BPS Books (The British Psychological Society), St Andrews House, 48 Princess Road East, Leicester LE1 7DR, UK.

ISBN 1 85433 231 7

Typeset by Poole Typesetting (Wessex) Limited
Printed in Great Britain by Antony Rowe Ltd, Chippenham, Wiltshire

CONTENTS

List of contributors

Fiona Barlow-Brown, Department of Psychology, University of Southampton, Highfield, Southampton S09 5NH, UK.

Rachel Brown, Department of Psychiatry, University of Alabama at Birmingham and Children's Hospital, Birmingham, Alabama, AL 35294, USA.

Glyn M. Collis, Department of Psychology, University of Warwick, Coventry CV4 7AL, UK.

Alan Fogel, Department of Psychology, University of Utah, Salt Lake City, UT 84112, USA.

Margaret Harris, Department of Psychology, University of London, Egham Hill, Egham, Surrey TW20 0EX, UK.

R. Peter Hobson, Developmental Psychopathology Research Unit, The Tavistock Clinic, 120 Belsize Lane, London NW3 5BA, UK.

Barbara Landau, Department of Psychology, University of Delaware, Newark, Delaware, DE 19716, USA.

Anthony Lee, Developmental Psychopathology Research Unit, The Tavistock Clinic, 120 Belsize Lane, London NW3 5BA, UK.

Vicky Lewis, Centre for Human Development and Learning, School of Education, Open University, Milton Keynes MK7 6AA, UK.

John L. Locke, Department of Human Communication Sciences, University of Sheffield, 18a Claremont Place, Sheffield S10 2TA, UK.

Susanna Millar, Department of Experimental Psychology, South Parks Road, University of Oxford, Oxford OX1 3UD, UK.

Margaret E. Minter, Child and Family Consultation Service, Oxleas NHS Trust, Chevening Road, Greenwich, London SE10 0LB, UK.

Gunilla Preisler, Department of Psychology, Stockholm University, S-10691 Stockholm, Sweden.

Susan L. Recchia, Department of Curriculum and Teaching, Teachers College, Columbia University, 525 W. 120th Street, New York, NY 10027, USA.

This book is dedicated to the memory of
Mary Kitzinger

Preface

This book has three aims. The first is to encourage dialogue between those interested in the process of psychological development through the study of typically developing children and those interested in the psychological development of children who are blind. Implicit within this is the goal of identifying key points of connection between the development of children with disabilities and contemporary developmental psychology. Four areas of development are considered: conceptual and linguistic development; reading and related skills; social and emotional development; and autistic-like behaviour. Making links is enabled by including two chapters on each area of development: one by researchers working with children who are blind, and the second by researchers interested in the area of development as a result of studying typically developing children or children with disabilities other than blindness. Together, these pairs of chapters provide insights into the contributions of studies of both typically developing children and children with disabilities to our understanding of psychological development.

The second aim of the book is to identify and examine issues which are likely to form the basis of developments in the field of early visual impairment up to and beyond the turn of the century. This has been achieved by selecting authors who are at the forefront of research into the development of blind children within each of the four areas.

The third aim of the book is to make recent developments in thinking about psychological development in general, and development of blind children in particular, accessible to practitioners. The contributors to the book are psychologists rather than practitioners; however, many of the ideas which are presented in the chapters have clear implications for practice. In particular, all the chapters provide insights into the processes of psychological development, and should be of interest to practitioners working with young children whether or not the children are typically developing, have a visual impairment or some other sort of disability.

Thus, although the main focus of the book is blindness and some of the specific points which are made will be relevant only to children with severe visual impairments, many of the issues which are raised within the book are directly relevant to understanding psychological development in general.

Most of the chapters were originally presented as papers at a symposium funded by the Mary Kitzinger Trust. This Trust was set up in the memory of Mary Kitzinger, a child psychotherapist, with the objective of advancing education, training and research in the psychology of children with visual and other developmental disabilities, as well as fostering communication between child psychologists, paediatricians, psychotherapists and others. We are very grateful for the support of the Mary Kitzinger Trust which enabled us to bring to fruition the idea of actively making links between the study of the development of blind children and mainstream developmental psychology.

There are ten chapters in the book. The first chapter, by Vicky Lewis and Glyn Collis, introduces a number of issues which are relevant to the study of children with severe visual impairments and to the aim of relating these findings to our understanding of development in general. The chapter considers how studies of special populations can contribute to our understanding and how research findings from such populations may be incorporated into theories of development. It also addresses a number of methodological issues including whether it is appropriate to use paradigms developed with typically developing children with children with disabilities; the problem of individual differences; and the question of whether it is possible to equate differ-ent groups of children in any meaningful way.

The next two chapters consider conceptual and linguistic develop-ment. In the first of these, Barbara Landau considers the development of blind children, examining how blind children might identify the meanings of particular words, especially nouns, which refer to objects, and verbs, which refer to actions. She suggests that aspects of noun and verb meaning are available to blind (and sighted) children through the structure of language or syntax itself, in contrast to the view that at least some words involve visual experience and that therefore certain concepts will be meaningless to a blind child. She also argues that the view that the blind child's early vocabulary is more tied to context and is generalized less than that of the sighted child may reflect the use of measures which fail to take account of how the blind child experiences his or her environment. She argues that researchers need to develop appropriate methodological tools to assess equivalent developments in children who are unable to see.

The second chapter of this pair is by John Locke, who broadens the debate to developmental psychology in general. He argues that we need to discard our biases about the role of vision in psychological development, and emphasizes the potential for compensation that exists. Commenting on the highly figurative nature of our language, Locke asks, why should 'the trees are green' mean less to those without sight than 'policemen are our friends' means to sighted children?

The next pair of chapters consider the development of reading in blind and sighted children. One way in which blind children clearly differ from sighted children is that they are likely to learn how to read braille. But how similar is the process of reading braille to that of reading print, since, although it is linguistically identical to print, it differs in terms of its physical format, the intake of information during movement of the fingers rather than when the fingers are stationary, and in some aspects of its orthography? This is a question posed by

Susanna Millar who suggests similar phonological effects in braille as those observed in children reading print. The second chapter on reading is by Margaret Harris and Fiona Barlow-Brown, who also examine the similarities and differences between blind and sighted children in the various strategies used to read braille and print.

The third set of papers considers social and emotional development. In many ways the social and emotional development of young children with severe visual impairments are similar to those of children who can see. However, in the absence of vision, the child relies on auditory and tactile information and, as a result, will have fewer opportunities to discover the interpersonal rules of communication, the relationships between objects and symbols, and knowledge about the surrounding environment. These restrictions result in difficulties for blind children in sharing meanings with others, which become more evident if the children are involved in pre-school activities with sighted children. In her chapter, Gunilla Preisler focuses on the nature of the interpersonal encounters between blind children and parents, peers and teachers from infancy to early adolescence. She points out that despite the significance attributed to children's friendships and the acknowledged difficulties that blind children experience in forming friendships, very little is done practically to help blind children develop the skills necessary to enable them to interact successfully with their peers. She urges those working with blind children to shift their focus away from performance measures of blind children towards a focus on the blind child forming relations with his or her social environment.

In the second paper on social and emotional development, Alan Fogel notes that vision is just one of several sensory avenues and that blind children can compensate and adapt effectively to a sightless world. He points out that this non-visual world is a world shared by us all but rarely touched upon by the sighted population. He argues that vision is heavily integrated into our social order and this may be as much a cause of the difficulties faced by those without sight as blindness itself. Claiming that individual and cultural differences reflect the availability of both visual and non-visual worlds, Fogel speculates that cultures which emphasize physical interaction may be more beneficial for the emotional development of blind children.

Many researchers and practitioners have commented that some children with severe visual impairments exhibit a number of behaviours which are reminiscent of those characteristic of children with autism. This is the topic considered in the next pair of chapters. Peter Hobson and colleagues demonstrate that, although there is a high prevalence of autistic-like features in congenitally blind children, the autistic-like behaviours in these children do differ in certain ways from those seen in sighted children with autism. They discuss the implications of these and other findings, including studies of symbolic play in blind children, for theories of development. Susan Recchia in her chapter discusses these issues within the conceptual framework of intersubjectivity and suggests compensatory processes which may facilitate these aspects of development in blind children.

The final chapter in the book, by Glyn Collis and Vicky Lewis, reflects on the issues raised in the first chapter in the light of the views expressed and the evidence cited in the eight intervening chapters. They consider in particular the implications for theories of developmental psychology, ways of studying children with and without disabilities, ways of aiding the development of children with disabilities, and point to areas where more research is needed.

One of the reasons for putting together this collection of chapters, and one of the motivating factors behind the original symposium where many of the ideas were first presented, is to emphasize the importance of research and practice starting from the child with a disability and her or his experience, rather than assuming, as has often been the case, that research methods and practices developed with typically developing children can be applied with little or no modification to children with disabilities. We hope that the chapters in this book will convince you of the importance of this. We also hope that the book will contribute to bridging the gap between theoretical research and clinical practice, as well as to our understanding of the psychological processes underlying development.

Vicky Lewis and Glyn M. Collis

Methodological and theoretical issues associated with the study of children with visual impairment

Vicky Lewis and Glyn M. Collis

Information received through the visual system is often taken for granted by those of us who can see. Visual information guides many of our actions, helping us to avoid colliding with objects and other people, and enabling us to make sense of the environment around us. We use many visual terms in our everyday language. Our interactions with other people rely on visual feedback. Our access to written material is dependent upon our ability to see print. And so on; the list is endless. However, although sighted people may take for granted a fundamental role of visual information in their everyday functioning, it is important to consider whether or not such information is really essential. In the absence of vision, can people make sense of, and talk about, their environment and interact successfully with both objects and people? Those of us who know someone who cannot see, especially someone who has never been able to see, know that people without vision can be as capable at interacting with their world as people who can see. This raises questions about how the skills involved in successfully interacting with the world develop in children who are without sight, and how the development of these skills can be facilitated. Addressing these questions will raise more general issues about the role of vision in psychological development.

The study of children who cannot see is important for both theoretical and practical reasons. Many theories of development seem to assume that information available to the developing child through the visual modality is primary, and that, in the absence of such information, certain developments will not occur. This is perhaps best illustrated by considering the development of language and a conceptual framework for understanding space. Our language contains a number of terms which seem to depend entirely on vision, such as colour labels, descriptions of objects, such as the moon, which can be seen but which are too far away to experience in any other way, and terms defining relationships between distant objects, such as their position and movement relative to one another. It may seem self-evident that being unable to see will have profound implications for the development of these aspects of mind. However, a theme that runs through all the following chapters is that empirical evidence shows that the influence of blindness on psychological development is nowhere near such a straightforward issue as might appear from mere reflection on the issue. This will be taken up again in Chapter 10.

The study of children with severe visual impairments raises a number of important issues also arising in the study of children with other kinds of disability that alter the way in which they make sense of their environment. A number of these issues are considered in the rest of this chapter.

Why study children with disabilities?

One reason for studying children with a disability such as blindness is the expectation that a better understanding of how the disability affects development should lead to more appropriate intervention aimed at improving the developmental progression of these children. However, the payoff should not stop there, for advances in our understanding of development in blind children should feed back into our understanding of more general issues in psychological development.

The study of children with disabilities can inform theories of developmental processes in a number of ways. For example, the findings may provide confirmation or disconfirmation that certain developments are prerequisite for later developments, generating new hypotheses about interdependencies among developmental achievements. The findings may help to elucidate the relationships between different areas of development, showing perhaps that although the behaviours usually emerge at the same time in typically developing children, they are actually independent. It may also become clear that certain aspects of psychological functioning have been given too much prominence in accounts of development, to the detriment of others.

In these and other ways, the study of children with disabilities can test many of the assumptions underlying accounts of developmental processes and can therefore make an important contribution to our understanding of development. Enhancements to our theories of psychological development will feed back to theory and practice concerned with the development of children with disabilities. Well-founded practice should not be based solely on either observations of children who have a particular disability, or on inferences from our understanding of normal development. Intervention should be based on an understanding of developmental processes which takes account of the full range of developmental achievements and the many developmental pathways available. Similarly, the outcome of practice will also contribute to the broader developmental account, in that an intervention which is based on particular principles or assumptions provides a test of those principles or assumptions, and must necessarily be fed back into the account.

Thus the study of children with disabilities can contribute not only to practice but also to theory, and this interplay between theory and practice is of vital importance for advancing our understanding of development.

How should explanations of the development of children with disabilities be related to those of children who are developing normally?

It is much simpler to state the ideal of an interplay between an understanding based on studies of children with disabilities and that arising from studies of typically developing children than it is to implement it. The pragmatics of integrating evidence from research into the development of normally developing children, and evidence on the development of children with one or other of various types of disability, make this a formidable task. In practice, the overall problem has to be segmented into parts to make it tractable, and some approaches to this segmentation problem are more satisfactory than others.

The simplest approach is to assemble different accounts of psychological development for each type of disability and one for children who have no disability. This is the default situation, since it corresponds to the segmentation of academic and professional allegiances and career structures. However, this approach does little to facilitate the cross-fertilization of ideas underlying the analyses of development in different groups of children. In particular, it provides little opportunity of testing hypotheses and assumptions which might be made in accounts which only relate to the study of typically developing children (and vice versa). A further limitation is that because more research involves children who are developing normally than children with disabilities, theories which account for normal development are likely to be seen as the basis from which all other developmental theory stems.

A partial advance on this 'separate explanations' approach is to draw together accounts of psychological development in children with a range of disabilities, still keeping this distinct from the account of development in normal children. However, this 'half-way house' has a number of major limitations. The account of development in children with disabilities will tend to highlight the things they have in common, which might lead to an overemphasis on general factors, such as low expectations and impoverished experience, at the expense of specific issues and the possibility of alternative developmental pathways which are unlikely to be the same for different disabilities. Moreover, the disabled/not disabled distinction is likely to lead to conclusions which emphasize differences between children who have disabilities and those who do not.

A third approach is to segment the overall problem according to domains of psychological development, such as spatial cognition, language, social relationships, and so on. Within each domain, similarities and differences can be examined between different types of disability and normal development. The main drawback is that development within a particular domain does not occur independently of developments in other areas. Once again, it can be seen that if developmental accounts do not take notice of all that is going on in development in both children with disabilities and children without disabilities, the resulting explanations will not be comprehensive. An account which encompasses all areas of development in all children should be what we are aiming for.

Where and how to start: with the typically developing child or with the child with a disability?

The adoption of one sort of theory of development or another has important implications for how we approach the study of the development of children with disabilities. In the last section it was argued that separate theoretical accounts may lead to the development of the child without any disabilities being seen as the starting point. This raises the question of whether the normal course of development should be taken as a benchmark for development in the presence of disabilities. If this is done, methodologies and paradigms developed in the study of normal development will be applied to the study of development in children with disabilities, which may be inappropriate. The behaviour subjected to scrutiny may also be inappropriate, beyond highlighting what *cannot* be done by children with a particular kind of disability. This makes it quite difficult to recognize alternative routes of development. For example, consider the resistance to accepting the sign language of the deaf as a real language, and hence as an alternative route to the development of presumed linguistically-based processes.

The alternative is to start with children with a disability, and to try to understand the upper levels of accomplishment in a particular domain and then seek to understand the development of these accomplishments. This can be compared with the course and processes of development of analogous behaviours in normally developing children, but unfettered by the presumption that the appropriate end point for development is what is achieved by normally developing children. The way in which we study children with disabilities is bound to be influenced by what we know about development in children who are developing normally, but by deliberately starting by observing the child with a disability in his or her own environment and talking to those who know the child well, it is likely that we shall identify developments which might otherwise be overlooked if we restricted our study to phenomena seen in children without disabilities.

Such an approach is also likely to result in the development of more appropriate methodologies which take account of the likely effect of the disability on development.

Should the development of children with disabilities be compared to the development of other children?

Traditionally, conclusions about the development of children with disabilities are based on observations of how they perform on a particular task in comparison to the performance of children who differ from them in specified ways. For example, the performance of children with autism has been compared to that of children with a different disability, such as Down's syndrome, but of similar developmental and chronological ages, and also to that of typically developing children of a similar developmental age but who are necessarily younger chronologically.

Such comparisons are justified in a number of different ways. For example, the comparison between children with autism and children with Down's syndrome is assumed to indicate whether or not any differences between the children with autism and the typically developing children are specific to autism or a function of a more general learning difficulty. However, it is important to ask whether such comparisons are always meaningful. In particular, it may be that the children in the different groups behave differently, not because they differ with respect to the ability under investigation, but because the methodology used does not allow all the groups to demonstrate that ability to the same extent. In other words, it may be necessary to use different methodologies to take account of the effects of different disabilities. Alternatively, it may be the case that although the overt behaviour or performance which is observed in the children in the different groups is similar, the processes underlying these abilities may not be the same. That is, the similarity of the overt behaviour may be misleading in terms of the underlying processes.

Often comparison groups can only be matched on one particular measure and then not perfectly, and yet we want to draw conclusions which are very dependent upon supposed clear similarities between the groups. Children with some sort of disability involving a learning difficulty may be compared to normal children who are younger but supposedly functioning at a similar level. But because these children are younger they may approach the task in a very different way from the older, but, for their age, less able, children. Similarly, children with different disabilities may be compared, and conclusions based on any differences observed, and yet the groups of children may differ from each other in many more ways than they are similar.

Psychology has a tradition of making comparisons between different groups of participants, and very often these are informative. But what is important to consider, particularly when studying the development of children with disabilities, is whether at least as much can be learnt (and possibly more) by simply observing the children who have the disability. If it is decided that additional information about developmental processes can be gained by including one or more comparison groups, very careful consideration needs to be made of which groups are appropriate – whether it should be children with another disability and/or typically developing children, and how the groups of children should be matched.

How similar are children who have the same disability?

This tradition of making comparisons between groups who differ from one another in specified ways enables statements to be made about general differences between groups by using the group data to iron out any marked individual differences. However, this strategy embodies the assumption that the individuals who make up each group are similar to one another in crucial respects and are different from all the other individuals in the comparison group in terms of other specified aspects. This assumption looks extremely dubious in the context of studies of individual differences in normal development, and case study reports of children with disabilities.

The grounds for grouping children with disabilities together vary. They may be grouped together because they have the same diagnosis based on the presence of a specific medical condition. Probably the clearest example of this is children with Down's syndrome, where all the children share the same chromosomal condition. Other children may be grouped together because they have the same functional disability, although the underlying aetiologies may vary. An example here would be children who are all totally blind, but for different reasons. Children may also be grouped together because they have been given a clinical diagnosis based on the presence of a critical number of characteristic behaviours, although the underlying medical condition and cause of the disability may be unclear and may differ between children. A relevant example here would be autism. A fourth way of grouping children with disabilities is on the basis of their performance on specific psychometric tests. In this case, an example would be children identified as having learning difficulties who perform at, or below, a particular level on a test of intelligence. Such a group may contain children whose disabilities are due to a whole range of different causes, some of which will have been identified, others of which will be unknown.

All the examples given in the preceding paragraph can be found within the research literature concerned with the psychological development of children with disabilities. In all cases, the emphasis is on the ways in which the individuals within each group are *similar* to one another, and little or no attention is usually paid to the ways in which the children within any one group may *differ* from one another. And yet even within a group of children who share the same medical condition, such as Down's syndrome, there may be a great deal of variation in terms of psychological functioning. In groups where the similarity between the members is based simply on their performance on a psychometric test, the possibilities for variation are even greater.

Thus, as a result of the nature of many disabilities, children who make up a so-called group may bear very little similarity to one another. Although they may be similar to one another with respect to a crucial factor, be it their medical diagnosis, their functional diagnosis, their clinical diagnosis or some specific psychometric performance, it is important to ask whether grouping children who are similar in some way, but who necessarily differ from each other in many ways, can throw much light on the process of development. Clearly, where the behaviour of a particular group of children differs markedly from the behaviour of another group of children something useful may be concluded. However, where the differences are slight or where there are no differences it is very difficult to draw firm conclusions.

Looking at individual children

Given the difficulties associated with grouping children with disabilities in meaningful ways it is perhaps not surprising that accounts of the development of individual children with particular disabilities are often especially illuminating. One of the main advantages of such case studies is that the observer is not channelled into making comparisons with other children in other groups and so is much more likely to focus attention on the child and his or her development rather than on how that child differs from, or is similar to, other children. Such studies can be very important in identifying overlooked areas of development and alternative routes. It might then be appropriate to see how well-represented these observations are within the population of children who have the same disability.

In all of this it is important to remember that differences between children, even if they have the same underlying problem, can tell us as much about the processes underlying development, as the similarities between children. Developmental psychology must be able to explain both similarities and differences in development, although in published research the emphasis is very much on explaining differences *between* groups with less emphasis on explaining differences *within* groups.

Conclusions

This chapter has discussed a number of issues which are highly pertinent to the study of children with disabilities. Many of them are addressed in the following chapters which consider findings from the development of children with severe visual impairments and points of contact between findings from a population of children with a disability and theoretical accounts of psychological development. Although the chapters which follow focus primarily on children with severe visual impairments, many of the issues discussed are relevant to the study of children with all types of disability.

Chapter Two

Language and experience in blind children: retrospective and prospective

Barbara Landau

The focus of this chapter is language learning in blind children, in particular the theoretical questions that are raised and can be answered by studying this population; the practical problems faced by blind children learning language; and some of the solutions that can be brought to bear on these problems. The issues raised by the study of blind children are classical ones in the philosophical and psychological study of the human mind. During the twentieth century, studies of the blind have had two primary foci. One continues the classical tradition, asking questions about the origins and nature of human development: does the development of knowledge originate with sensory or perceptual experience? Or is the character of knowledge separate from the particulars of experience? The second focus leads to somewhat different questions concerning the pragmatic problems that blind children might encounter during early development: What are the practical consequences of being blind, and how do these affect development?

The two sets of questions can be logically separated, although investigators do not always do so. Doing so, however, is critical in order to fully understand how blind children learn. The aim of this chapter is not to provide complete answers to questions about the origins and nature of human knowledge, nor to completely explain how blind children learn language. Rather, it is to try to disentangle some important issues concerning blind children's language learning. In so doing, the goal is to point the way towards the kinds of research that will enable real progress to be made in understanding both the nature of knowledge and the kinds of experience that can promote learning by blind and sighted children alike.

The empiricist perspective

The question of how the blind child learns language has a long history, of course, framed as part of a general inquiry into the nature and origins of human knowledge. For empiricists such as Bishop Berkeley (1709), John Locke (1690), and David Hume (1758), the case of the blind served as a touchstone for considering the nature of human knowledge, and how it is acquired. This was because the empiricists considered sensory experience to play a central role in the acquisition of knowledge. For Berkeley, who was most concerned with perception and understanding of space, it followed logically that if spatial perception and knowledge originated in sensory input, then qualitative differences in the experience from different sensory modalities would inevitably lead to qualitative differences in the knowledge of space. Thus the blind person and the sighted person could never truly share the same understanding of space. For Locke and Hume, who were more concerned with the nature of human concepts – such as those encoded by the lexicon – the blind and sighted would also inevitably differ in the contents of their thoughts. This was because the presumed building blocks for concepts originated in the nervous system; again, because the empiricists considered sensory input to play a central causal role in the acquisition of concepts. They assumed there could never be true equivalences unless the avenues of experience were identical. Key cases here concerned the acquisition of strictly 'visual' terms by the blind, for example, the representation and acquisition of colour terms. The cases were key, because first, it seemed obvious to the empiricists that relevant aspects of experience were missing, and second, because the empiricists assumed that this particular experience, seeing colour, was causal in the development of the understanding and use of words such as 'red' and 'blue'. If colour concepts become linked to colour words as a result of relevant sensory experiences, then the blind could never come to possess the same colour concepts as the sighted. Thus, quite strong assumptions were made by the empiricists about the nature and role of experience in learning: sensory experience played a central causal role in the acquisition of concepts.

The nativist perspective

From a very different perspective, nativists have asked the same questions, but have come up with very different answers. Relevant challenges from nativists have been made on two grounds. First, nativists have objected that sensory input is not causally related to the acquisition of knowledge for anyone, whether blind or sighted. As Fodor

(1981) has pointed out, the classical empiricist programme still remains the most defensible and coherent on the issue of what actually constitutes the building blocks of knowledge (the sensory primitives). However, there is no evidence that lexical concepts such as 'dog', 'house', or 'run' can be broken down into such basics. Once one opens up the possibility of so-called higher-level basics, Fodor argues, there is no reason why one should not make the claim that all lexical concepts such as 'dog', 'house', 'run', and so on, are primitives themselves. In sum, from a logical and empirical point of view, the original empiricist programme is likely to be false.

A second challenge from nativists comes from observations on the nature of human language and its acquisition; together these led nativists to emphasize the problem of learning from impoverished input. For example, although part of the mature system of human language requires representations of lexical categories such as noun, verb, adjective, and structurally-defined categories such as subject and object, there is nothing apparent in the environment that could reflect these categories and play a direct causal role in their acquisition. Furthermore, nativists have tended to emphasize the rapidity and error-free nature of language acquisition and its robustness under widely varying environmental and social/cultural conditions. Within an enormous range of intellectual potential, whether they are born hearing or deaf, whether they are raised in privileged or less privileged environments, children learn language within the first few years. This suggests to the nativist that the child's relevant experience must provide nourishment for categories that are privileged or, in the strongest form, pre-wired.

Environmental influence

Of course, no nativist would claim that language is learned in a vacuum. The very fact that the language of the surrounding community is the language that one learns proves that language learning depends strongly on environmental input, that of hearing one's native language. Given recent findings in developmental biology, it seems clear that the relationship between innate blueprints and experience is both complex and variable, depending on the area in question. For example, a century ago it was assumed that having a genetic programme necessarily meant that it was unmodifiable; that is, that the environment could have no real effect. However, we now know differently. In the case of phenylketonuria (PKU), a specific genetic defect that results in the absence of certain enzymes required to metabolize phenylalanine, the behavioural effects of PKU, namely severe retardation, can be avoided by simple alterations in the environment. Specifically, if babies with PKU are placed on diets restricted in phenylalanine, they develop quite normally. Thus, having a genetically-specified component to development does not rule out effects of the environment; quite the contrary, the genetically-specified component must be realized in the context of some particular environment.

Thus the nativist answer to questions about the nature and role of experience in language learning emphasizes the rich structure of the system to be acquired and its robustness over a wide variety of experiential conditions. However, it also raises the very important question of what constitutes the experience that is required to realize the system of knowledge, and how that experience succeeds in modulating the existing structure. It is here, on the issue of what constitutes experience and what role it plays, that nativists part company with empiricists most strongly. Whereas classical empiricists assumed that experience could be characterized as sensory primitives and that these played a causal role in learning, nativists have assumed that experience must be biased by existing structure or units and that experience does not cause learning, but rather *triggers* learning. To be fair, most modern empiricists (for example, Mandler, 1992) do not view experience as limited to sensory primitives; in fact, the range of primitives or building blocks is astonishingly broad, including higher-level elements of concepts, social conditions, and so forth. The problem is that these additional elements of experience have never been so precisely described as in the classical empiricist programme; nor have they ever been so tidily linked to learning. Yet, grand conclusions have been drawn because of assumptions that are made about the necessary link between a certain kind of experience, specifically visual experience, and knowledge. This is not a 'straw man' argument. Consider the following quote from Dunlea (1989):

For many events, blind children are at a considerable disadvantage in terms of the information available. For example, consider the event encoded by the sentence 'George rolls the ball to Mary'. A sighted child . . . commenting on this is likely to encode 'ball', 'ball roll' or even 'George roll ball' . . . Now consider this from the blind child's perspective. If Mary is blind, she has immediate knowledge of her own existence and she can discover, after the ball has made contact with her, that the object in question is a ball . . . The concept 'roll (to)' is *virtually meaningless* for a blind child. Mary may come to recognize a *contingency* relationship between hearing a ball roll and the ball's bumping into her, but this is unreliable since the ball can miss its mark or be directed to someone other than herself. Clearly Mary could never experience an object's rolling action or understand its trajectory. Finally, Mary can be TOLD that George caused the ball to contact her, or she can infer it, but she cannot *know* it on her own' (p. 103, italics added).

This quote will be referred to later, but suffice it to say that the empiricist programme is alive and well, and that within this programme, at least some investigators hold that knowing the meanings of at least some words involves visual experience.

Why study language learning in blind children?

With these issues in mind, one might ask what contribution might be made by studying language learning in blind children? The global question of whether language is innate or learned is far too coarse. We know that there is a blueprint for language learning, and we also know that certain aspects of the child's experience, such as being exposed to a native language, are essential for fully realizing that blueprint. But given that the blind child's experience is not identical to that of the sighted child, understanding language learning in the blind child might help us understand more fully what, exactly, is the character of the critical experience.

It is with these two questions in mind – what constitutes experience in language learning, and how this experience is related to knowledge of language that both blind and sighted children acquire – that I would like to consider what we know and what we would *like* to know about language learning in the blind. Research indicates that experience is much more subtle than the empiricists ever imagined, and that the relationship between experience and knowledge is more subtle and complex than many nativists have thought (Landau and Gleitman, 1985). However, this same research and conclusions also raise many new questions about how blind or sighted children learn language, and these questions are well worth pursuing in future empirical studies of language learning.

Specificity of effects: Where are there differences?

Are there specific effects of blindness on language learning and, if so, what are they? First, consider the very general hypothesis that blindness has an effect on the child's ability to learn the combinatorial structure of language itself, the syntax. In fact, there have been several studies of blind children's acquisition of syntax (see Mills, 1983), and it has never been reported that the blind child has difficulty learning the syntactic structure of his or her native language. Further, as far as is known, the growth of syntax in blind children occurs roughly on time and develops normally (Landau and Gleitman, 1985). That is, nouns and verbs are acquired, their morphology and syntactic frames are acquired, and there are few anomalies. Some (for example, Andersen, Dunlea and Kekelis, 1984) have suggested that blind children exhibit a disproportionate number of imitative routines: in the extreme, this is called *echolalia*. However, there is no evidence that blind children, who are otherwise unimpaired, actually become stuck at this point in language learning. Moreover, sighted children vary a great deal in the degree to which they imitate language (Bloom, Lightbown and Hood, 1975), and this variation does not seem to have an impact on their ultimate learning of their native language.

The fact of normal syntactic acquisition might appear to miss what seems to be the most central problem for the language learner who is blind. Perhaps one can acquire syntax without access to meaning. Almost all theorists assume that the learner must have form–meaning pairings to learn a language, since language encodes the relationship between form and meaning. But perhaps the blind child could operate like some current connectionists models (such as Elman, 1993), by simply analysing the distributional regularities in the speech stream: that is, which words co-occur (precede and follow) which other words. These models do realize some modest generalization from old strings to new ones, although there is no obvious way in which they have learned to map structure onto meanings that are connected to observations in the world. The consequences for such a learner would be only modest generalization, possibly not beyond certain basic syntactic facts holding for one or two-clause sentences and no obvious connection between what is observed and meaning.

The difference between these models and any human language learner is that the human produces and comprehends utterances that are both meaningful and novel. The child learns not only which words co-occur with which other words, but what these words mean and what the different combinations of words mean. The child learner (but not the connectionist model) understands when it is appropriate to say 'The dog bit the cat', rather than 'The cat bit the dog'. It would seem, then, that the child learner is learning the mapping between forms and meanings, not just well-formed sequences of forms.

So what do we make of the acquisition of syntax by the blind child? The best guess right now is that the blind child's language is meaningful, but that there may be problems in connecting the referents of the blind child's language to the listener's construction of what is being said. This will be discussed further later in the chapter.

Consider now some of the basic aspects of meaning required to put together the syntax.

Form–meaning relationships

In order to learn the word order of one's input language and connect it with meaning (which is what word order actually does, after all), the learner needs to identify which words in the sentences are the subjects, verbs, and objects, and what thematic (semantic) roles the subjects and objects play with respect to the verb. For example, for the sentence 'John gave a cake to Mary', the learner must recognize that 'John' is the agent and subject, 'a cake' is the patient and direct object, and "Mary' the recipient and indirect object. This undoubtedly requires learning since the child cannot automatically tell whether the language heard is Subject–Verb–Object (SVO) or Subject–Object–Verb (SOV). How does the child, blind or sighted, determine which words are the subjects, which are the verbs, and which are the objects, in advance of knowing the word order?

Theorists have proposed that the child begins by a kind of bootstrapping from observations of the world to the words in a sentence (see Pinker, 1989, for a review). According to Grimshaw (1981), all children may assume first that names for objects are nouns, and that names for actions are verbs (or other relational terms). Further, they may make assumptions about the mappings between nouns and different thematic roles, which in turn map onto syntactic categories such as subject and object. Children might assume, for instance, that the role of agent maps onto subject and the role of patient maps onto direct object. With these assumptions, one could determine which noun was the subject and which the indirect object, thus establishing the language's basic word order. In fact, a child may need to know as little as which words are the nouns. Then, by default (and using certain universal principles of syntax), the remaining elements could be inferred to constitute the verb and its complements.

Note that in order for this scheme to work, the burden of explanation has been placed on understanding how the child identifies, initially, from his or her observations, the nouns and the verbs. Since this is proposed to be accomplished initially by observations, this could be the locus of the blind child's problem. It might be predicted that this could be difficult for the blind child, who would seem to have access to less rich information through which to identify the particular objects and actions that map onto particular nouns and verbs. Although these have been treated as a uniform problem, the two parts of the problem, namely the acquisition of nouns and verbs by bootstrapping from objects and actions, may require very different solutions.

The fact is, blind children do not appear to have difficulty learning the syntax of their native language, nor speaking in sentences that have meaning. This indicates one of two things about the role of visual experience in the acquisition of language. One possibility is that interpretations of heard sentences are not critical in the construction of syntax. This seems doubtful, as language comprises the mappings between form and meaning, and blind children, like sighted children, produce new combinations of words that have unique meanings. Alternatively, it is possible that the mechanisms of mapping meaning and form for both blind and sighted children are considerably more subtle and complex than previously imagined. If this is correct, it would suggest the need to refine our ideas about the nature of the experience required to learn a language.

The acquisition of nouns and noun meanings

In order to discover which words are the nouns, the blind child, like the sighted child, has two routes. One is to use the form class cues to identify nouns. For example, if the child knows that nouns can be preceded by determiners (in English, 'a', 'an', 'the') and/or quantifiers ('some', 'much', 'many', numbers), then she or he could identify the nouns as those words that follow a specific class of words (the determiners in English). Numerous studies have shown that by the age of about two, sighted children can use such syntactic contexts to learn novel nouns. For example, Katz, Baker and Macnamara (1974) showed that 24-month-old girls could use the syntactic distinction between common and proper nouns to learn a new noun and extend it properly. When children were shown a novel doll, and told 'This is a dax', they later generalized the noun 'dax' to other dolls. But when subjects of the same age were shown the same novel doll, and told 'This is Dax', they later restricted the noun 'Dax' to only the doll they were shown, suggesting that they had inferred that Dax was the doll's name. Because proper names cannot be generalized to other objects on the basis of similarity, the children restricted the name to the original doll. Use of such cues, like the existence and nature of the determiners accompanying the target noun, presupposes that young children at the beginning of word learning can, in fact, detect these cues.

Since many children at the early stages of language learning speak telegraphically, omitting many function words (for example, saying 'Throw ball', rather than 'Throw the ball'), one might think that using determiners to guide learning would be difficult or impossible. However, evidence suggests that even telegraphic speakers (who do not produce function words in their speech) nevertheless recognize the existence of determiners. Gerken, Remez, and Landau (1990) showed that telegraphic speakers selectively omitted *only* English functors from imitated strings, suggesting that they were processing these as a special group. Also, Bloom (1996) has pointed out that many early produced nouns do not refer to objects. Since abstract nouns would seem to require distributional (syntactic) evidence for learning, it is a good bet that young children who produce non-object nouns are indeed using syntactic and morphological information as a guide to learning these words. It would be surprising if the blind child could not also use such cues. It would be worth testing this hypothesis empirically in order to establish the usability of such syntactic information at the onset of language learning.

In the absence of such syntactic information at the very beginning of language learning, the blind or sighted child might use a second route. This route assumes a canonical mapping between object names and nouns; that is, the assumption that objects are named by nouns. It further assumes that the child can tell when someone is naming an object. Once the child hears an object name, he or she should identify it also as a noun. Once the child has heard the object's name, he or she will be able to generalize the name to other objects which are similar in relevant ways. Although such generalization does not typically begin to proliferate until children have acquired roughly 50 words, there is ample evidence among sighted children that they do generalize, sometimes producing quite salient errors in which what they call a 'horse' or a 'cup' does not exactly match the adult's extension (for example, Clark, 1973).

These two processes of linking objects with their names, and generalizing to other objects of the same kind, have been a focus of interest of language learning in the blind. There are two issues here. One is the extent to which blind infants suffer a deficit or delay due to their reduced opportunity to establish joint reference. That is, to the extent that the blind child cannot determine what object is actually being named by the speaker, he or she may well suffer delays in the acquisition of object names. The second issue follows more closely from the empiricist tradition, and questions the extent to which the blind child has the ability to develop object categories that are represented by words. Given this putative difficulty, the blind child might then fail to generalize in the same way and as freely, abstractly, and coherently, as the sighted child.

Establishing joint attention

First consider the issue of joint attention. It seems intuitively obvious that joint attention is most easily and naturally established in infancy through visual gaze. The fundamental properties of mutual gaze have been investigated by a variety of scientists including Collis (1977), Butterworth (1983) and Bruner (1974/1975). But what happens in the absence of gaze?

One obvious possibility is that the blind child and parent might be at a disadvantage in establishing reference. This does not mean that blindness inevitably leads to the inability to establish joint reference; indeed, a number of investigators have informally documented that the blind child and his or her parents can develop alternative means of establishing joint reference (Landau and Gleitman, 1985). For example, parents might bring the object of their attention into the blind child's line of attention by presenting the object to the child, and mutually holding or exploring it while naming it.

Despite these observations, however, we know little about the effectiveness of these alternative means, and the extent to which blind or sighted children develop the ability to use joint reference in language learning if they are given appropriate equivalent means of establishing joint reference. There are a number of important empirical and theoretical questions here. For example, at what age is the sighted (or blind) infant capable of actually using visual gaze (or alternative cues) to establish joint reference and to support the learning of a new word? This is an extremely important question, for the context of language learning is by no means perfect for the blind or sighted child: there are surely many occasions when the parent is talking about one thing while the infant's attention is directed elsewhere.

Baldwin (1991) has explored the ability of sighted infants to use visual cues to joint attention as a support for word learning. She has shown that by the age of about 16 months, the sighted child can use such cues in word learning, and that the child becomes much more adept, though by no means perfect, over the next three months. In Baldwin's experiment, infants were allowed to play with an interesting toy for several minutes. Then, an experimenter who was sitting with the infant named an object in one of two conditions. In the 'follow-in' labelling condition, the experimenter waited until the infant was looking at the toy she was playing with, then gazed at the same toy, and said, 'It's a peri'. In the 'discrepant' labelling condition, the experimenter waited until the infant was looking at the toy, then she looked straight into a bucket that contained a second toy (but was hidden from the infant's line of sight), and again said, 'It's a peri'. All infants participated in both conditions on different occasions. Half the infants were subsequently given a comprehension test in which they were shown both toys (the one they had played with and the one in the bucket) and asked, 'Show me the peri'. The other half of the infants were given a preference test in which they were shown both toys and asked, 'Which one do you like?' The question was whether infants were capable of taking advantage of the information from visual gaze: would they be more likely to link the object's name with the visible object when the experimenter was also gazing at it, that is, in the 'follow-in' labelling condition?

The results showed that 16–19 month-old infants did indeed select the visible toy more frequently in the 'follow-in' labelling condition. When the experimenter was gazing into the bucket, and uttered the sentence, 'It's a peri', the infants were less likely to connect that label to the object that was the focus of their attention. This suggests that infants at about one to one and a half years of age are sensitive to other people's line of sight information, and they can use this information to determine which objects are being talked about. Note, however, the sighted infants were by no means perfect. Even the 19-month-olds selected the visible toy only 72 per cent of the time in the 'follow-in' condition, and the same (visible) toy 34 per cent of the time in the 'discrepant' condition. This is important, for it shows that, despite the apparent transparency of visual gaze information, there will be many occasions on which the sighted child may err, either in making use of available information or in making assumptions about what the relevant information is.

What about the blind child? Clearly, she or he does not have this kind of line-of-sight information to take advantage of. In some sense, the blind child is in principle like the sighted infant who cannot distinguish between the follow-in and discrepant labelling conditions. This raises two questions, worthy of empirical pursuit. First, if given comparable, but non-visual, information about focus of attention, can the blind child take advantage of this information in word learning? Second, in the normal course of early development, what is the likelihood that a blind infant's mother or father actually does provide comparable information about their attentional focus? These are obviously two quite different questions, the first asking whether the blind child is in principle capable of using information about attentional focus; and the second asking whether in practice, the blind child actually receives comparable information. Once again, it should be noted that the situation for the sighted child is far from perfect: there will be many times when the adult labels an object that is not the focus of the infant's attention, and many times when the infant ignores information about the adult's line of sight. It would be well worth establishing the characteristics of the real empirical situation for the blind child, the nature of non-visual means of establishing mutual attention, and the extent to which he or she can make use of such information. To be more specific, one might ask what is the likelihood of the blind child actually learning the name of a novel object, under conditions that vary with respect to different kinds of information supporting joint reference.

Developing object categories

Turning to the issue of generalizing object names, studies of early vocabulary acquisition among sighted children have shown generalization of object names from fairly early on, although the earliest words learned are often context-bound or used only for specific objects encountered in specific situations (Bloom, 1973). However, one of the most salient characteristics of first language learners is their rapidly expanding vocabulary, and their propensity to generalize new words. The kind of underlying similarity governing these generalizations is currently an active area of research. Findings (Landau, Smith and Jones, 1988) indicate that young learners actively generalize object names on the basis of shape (a good indicator of category kind), and also that naming objects highlights their status as category members rather than as, say, participants in a thematic relationship (Markman and Hutchinson,1984; Waxman, 1994).

Although a number of studies have now shown that the content of early vocabulary in the blind and sighted is quite similar, some investigators still hold that a closer look reveals real differences. Dunlea (1989), who is a strong advocate of this position, noted the following differences between blind and sighted children (p. 61–62):

. . . no words acquired by the blind children were dropped from their lexicons whereas sighted children often discard terms which no longer *serve their needs* (italics added).

there were no idiosyncratic or child-created forms in the blind children's lexicons.

the blind children's words seem to be tied to their original context for a protracted period of time.

use of words for actions . . . describe their own activities or satisfy their own needs. They do not refer to the activities of others or encode information about the dynamic states of entities.

the process of lexical extension was very restricted in the blind children: 50–60 per cent of their first 100 words were not extended during the period of study . . . overextensions were rare in the blind children's lexicons (8–13 per cent), whereas sighted children overextend around one third of their first words (Rescorla, 1980).

no forms of class-consistent constructions or sorting behaviour were observed in either spontaneous play or structured classification tasks for the blind children.

Dunlea's conclusion, then, appears to be that the blind child's vocabulary is different from that of the sighted child in being more restricted to context, less freely generalizable, and possibly even disconnected from other indications that they understand category relations.

However, the evidence for such an interpretation is quite weak. First, it goes without saying that, without any rigorous definition of one's own needs, it would be impossible to actually determine whether this was a cause of preserving and/or discarding words. Moreover, there is no semantic theory that classifies words on the basis of personal use. Failure to drop words from the lexicon, failure to produce novel forms, and failure to overgeneralize are notoriously difficult to detect, even under conditions of continuous monitoring. Restriction of usage could easily be understood as a consequence of not having information that invites additional usage; the blind child encounters fewer round things so he or she is likely to generalize on the basis of roundness on a fewer number of occasions. Furthermore, evidence from sighted infants indicates that active over-generalization in production is not necessarily mirrored in comprehension (Huttenlocher, 1974). That is, children who spontaneously overgeneralize 'dog' to 'cat' do not necessarily think that 'dog' *means* 'cat'. Generally speaking, none of these is an indication that the vocabulary itself is impoverished in any deep way. In terms of non-linguistic classification, Dunlea's only measure was a sequential touching and grouping task that tends to elicit active exploration by sighted children. It would not be surprising if blind children were less able to show systematic sequential touching behaviour in such a task, for the blind might have the additional difficulty of keeping track of which objects have/have not been explored. This contrast by Dunlea is merely one instance among many serving as an urgent alarm: researchers interested in blind children's development must focus on developing suitable measures of early cognitive development, rather than relying on ones developed for the sighted. Clearly, one cannot claim lack of ability to categorize on the basis of tasks ill-suited for measuring such abilities in the first place.

The most that one can make of Dunlea's observations is that the blind child might have fewer opportunities to comment on objects and events observable to himself or herself and others. But it is critical to note that this is a separate question from whether the range or nature of the concepts underlying the early words of blind children is qualitatively different from that of the sighted.

There do exist many intriguing and important questions regarding the early nature of the blind child's object vocabulary. For example, evidence from sighted children (Markman and Hutchinson, 1984; Markman, 1989) shows that labelling objects for children appears to highlight their membership in taxonomic hierarchies, specifically, the labels that represent an object's kind. Children who hear novel objects labelled later tend to group these objects preferentially with other objects of like kind, very often objects of the same shape. In contrast, children who do not hear the objects named later tend to group the same objects along a variety of themes, including, for example, temporal proximity or thematic relatedness.

Does the label accomplish the same function for the blind child? Does the blind child know that an object's name represents its kind and that, once labelled, an object can be grouped together with other objects having the same label as members of the same category? What kinds of perceptual properties are most salient to the blind child as he or she groups objects? If shape is salient for the sighted child, perhaps serving as the best cue to the object kind, what is the equivalent for the blind child? Finally, once the blind child hears a pair of objects labelled with the same name, does he or she make the same range of inductive inferences about these objects as does the sighted child?

Such inferences, which do not depend in any straightforward way on the perceptual properties of objects are, according to many theorists, at the very heart of the human conceptual system (Gelman, 1988). For example, if someone introduces a new animal to you and tells you that it is a dog, then regardless of how much or how little it looks like dogs you've seen before, you are likely to assume that it shares many properties with other things called 'dog', that is, that it barks, wags its tail, lives with people, and so on. When we label a new object with a known term, we are prepared to infer that that completely novel object shares many properties with objects already assigned the term. This inductive power may be uniquely human; very likely it supports a variety of other knowledge-based activities. Inductive inference is a mental operation having nothing to do with the sensory and perceptual systems. As such, once the blind child makes contact with the world, and can co-refer, the infinite power of inference is at his or her fingertips.

The acquisition of verbs and verb meanings

Let us now consider verbs, their meanings, and their acquisition. In her 1989 monograph, Dunlea reports that the blind child's early sentences typically express events in which the child is the 'principal instigator or the possessor', and that novel information about objects, object attributes, and events is virtually absent. The evidence Dunlea offers for this conclusion is slim, relying principally on an analysis of semantic relations from the earliest stage of syntax, in which the blind children showed a sprinkling of the same semantic relations as the single sighted child studied. Dunlea suggests that blind children talk mostly about events they themselves experience – this is not surprising if they often cannot discern events in the larger context. Nevertheless, Dunlea's interpretation of these findings shows that she is convinced that one's knowledge is derived directly from one's experience. This was evident in the quote cited earlier in this chapter.

What Dunlea is proposing in that quote is that the blind child can never come to really know what 'rolling' means, and that this is why the blind child does not comment on balls rolling in the world. She apparently assumes that the meaning of the verb 'roll' can only be ascertained by visually observing balls rolling in the world.

This argument needs to be considered within the context of current theories of language learning. There are two central questions. First, how does the child learn the meaning of the verb 'roll', and second, how does he or she learn the syntactic structures in which the verb participates, for example, that one can say 'The ball rolled', or 'Mary rolled the ball', but not '*The ball rolled Mary', or '*Mary rolled the ball the boy', or '*Mary rolled that the ball went to George'.

According to recent theories (Gleitman, 1990), the solutions to these questions are intertwined. In the *semantic bootstrapping theory*

(Grimshaw, 1981), it is proposed that the child initially uses a mapping between objects and nouns on the one hand, and between actions and predicates on the other hand to determine which words in the speech stream are nouns and which are verbs. Once the child has determined this, he or she can learn the structures that accompany different verbs. This can be accomplished because, according to almost all modern theorists, verbs participate in certain syntactic structures by virtue of their meaning. For example, a verb such as 'roll' represents a particular manner of motion of an object. It can be caused motion (as when 'Mary rolls the ball to George'), or spontaneous motion (as when 'George rolls down the hill' or 'The balls rolls off the table due to gravity'). Because of its meaning, the verb must take at least one noun phrase (NP) argument, representing the entity that undergoes the motion of rolling. This is necessary under either caused or spontaneous motion. Taking the sentence 'The ball rolls', the subject NP is the theme of the verb roll. We can add more, however, for 'rolling' can also represent the motion of an object (the patient) caused by an agent; further, the direction and location can (optionally) be specified. In the sentence 'George rolls the ball', the agent George is the subject and the patient 'ball' is the direct object; in the sentence 'George rolls the ball to Mary', the same is true, with the addition of 'to Mary' which expresses the direction 'to' and the recipient 'Mary', the indirect object. So the verb 'roll' can appear in any of these three sentence frames. By virtue of what 'roll' means, it takes a minimum of one argument, and a maximum of three indicating agent, patient and location or recipient.

We can contrast this with a verb such as 'give', which represents the transfer of some entity from one person to another. Because of what 'give' means, it requires three arguments, one specifying the giver, one the entity given, and one the recipient. Sentences with 'give' require these three arguments: these include sentences such as 'George gave the ball to Mary', but not sentences such as 'The ball gave/George gave' or 'George gave the ball' or 'Gave the ball to Mary'. Thus, learning the meaning of the verb (so as to generalize appropriately) and learning the syntax of the verb (so as to generalize appropriately) are linked.

Returning to the semantic bootstrapping theory, the child hears the verb 'roll' as she or he observes something rolling or being rolled. Observing the motion called 'rolling', he or she then recognizes that such motion of an object must be encoded by a verb requiring at least one NP argument, to represent the ball, and another optional one in the case of externally caused motion, to represent the agent.

Now, whether or not this theory is correct (and it seems likely that it is at best *partially* correct for any child), it is necessary to ask what the blind child could be missing. As described, the verb 'roll' will take a maximum of three arguments: one representing the agent (or source), one the object, and one the recipient (or a location, as in 'Mary rolled the ball around the driveway').

In the agentive meaning ('Mary rolled the ball to George'), the child must be capable of observing that 'rolling' is a motion with a specific manner, caused by some agent, and having a separate destination. The identity of the agent and recipient might not be observable, unless the child him or herself is the agent or recipient. Of course, language could play a key role here, since the blind child can easily determine who is doing the rolling if he or she hears the name of the agent and/or recipient (and knows what sentential position should be occupied by these).

What about causality and trajectory? Causality is, of course, never embodied in the simple temporal sequence of events. Although Dunlea argues that the blind child can recognize a contingency relationship but not a causal one, it has long been recognized that causality is more than contingency, and that any unbiased observation, by the blind or sighted, can be read as either a mere temporal sequence or a causal one. However, the fact is that even infants seem to read certain events as causal, despite the fact that causality cannot be directly observed. Given this, there is no reason to suppose that the blind child is any less likely to read certain sequences as causal, and this includes sequences in which balls are rolled. As far as trajectory is concerned, although the blind child might not be able to observe certain trajectories, there will undoubtedly be plenty of occasions on which portions of the trajectory are observable: as the ball hits the child, as it rolls past the child's leg, as it bounces along the gravel driveway. Bigelow (1984) has shown that blind infants can make inferences about the paths of moving objects from partial information, just as sighted infants can. Finally, the manner of motion, the rolling part, can similarly be observed as the child is shown how to roll a ball, or feels it rolling across her or his body.

So, observational learning for blind children would not appear to be as impoverished as Dunlea supposes. But are such observations sufficient for any child, blind or sighted, to learn the meaning of the verb 'roll'? Consider the same scenario once more: Mary rolls the ball to George, someone says 'Mary rolled the ball to George', and the child observes what he or she can. Is it so obvious that the speech sound 'roll' means what we know it does? Or is it not also possible that the novel verb (for the child) could mean many other things: the speaker could be uttering the sentence 'Mary sends the ball to George', or 'George receives the ball from Mary,' or 'Look what a good ball player Mary is!'. The point is that observation by itself, even at its putative best, is not sufficient for the learner to determine exactly which of the many possible meanings the speaker has in mind. How, then, does the child learn which verb is the target one?

To address this problem, Landau and Gleitman (1985) first proposed that the child, blind or sighted, uses information from the syntactic contexts in which the verbs occur to help focus on the target meaning. This theory has been dubbed *syntactic bootstrapping* to emphasize the role of syntax in learning the meaning of verbs. Consider again the verb 'roll'. As already pointed out, 'roll' can occur with just one NP argument (in the case of spontaneous motion such as 'Mary rolled down the hill); it can occur with two NP arguments (in the case of caused motion, where 'Mary rolls the ball'); or it can occur with three arguments (where 'Mary rolls the ball to George'. Thus, if the child hears 'The ball xxx-s' and 'John xxx-s the ball', he or she will know that the verb 'xxx-s' occurs with a minimum of one argument, but that it can take two arguments. In the latter case, the child should know, based on his or her knowledge of the language, that the NP occupying the first place in this sentence is the agent and, therefore, that the verb must express a caused activity. If the child further hears 'John xxx-s the ball to Mary', he or she will know that the verb can also take propositional phrases (PP), which in English canonically express places and paths. These three frames are consistent with the general pattern for manner of motion verbs, hence the child will be able to infer that 'xxx-s' is a manner of motion verb.

It is important to note that there is nothing in the specific different frames that corresponds to the nature of rolling as distinct from sliding or throwing. This part of the meaning will have to be ascertained from some kind of observation. According to the semantic bootstrapping theory, if a large part of the meaning of the verb depends strictly on visual observations, it should be impossible for the blind child to learn the meaning of the verb. However, according to the syntactic bootstrapping theory, the child should be able to learn something about the meaning of the verb by determining which syntactic frames go with which verbs.

Is there any evidence that blind children have trouble learning the meanings of verbs, either in their appropriate contextual use, or in their syntactic contexts? Dunlea (1989) asserts that the blind children she studied used verbs in more restricted contexts than the sighted children, for example, only applying them to their own experiences. But this does not qualify as failure to learn the meaning of the verb in either the semantic or syntactic sense. Rather, it suggests that blind children may be less able to ascertain the occasions on which rolling, sliding, or throwing has occurred. Of course, learning only one or two of the appropriate occasions, together with learning the syntactic frames in which these verbs participate, should be sufficient for a full range of usage. To test this hypothesis in the extreme, Landau and Gleitman (1985) showed through extensive study of the semantic and syntactic use of visual verbs that the blind child was quite capable of learning even verbs such as 'look' and 'see', for which one might consider visual experience a necessary condition.

What does this mean? If syntax is a major contributing factor to the acquisition of verbs and verb meanings, then we might explain the similarity between blind and sighted children's verb acquisition in terms of an unimpaired system of syntax. The blind child, like the sighted child, can analyse the syntactic frames in which the verbs occur, and can thereby infer some of the elements of meaning for each verb. To the extent that contextual factors must also play a role in ascertaining the specific meaning of verbs such as roll, throw or slide, it is necessary to ask why it is that blind children, and blind adults for that matter, appear to be so comparable to the sighted. The answer must lie in a reconsideration of the kinds of experiences that really are critical to learning the meanings of verbs.

Conclusions

To summarize, studies of language learning in the blind have taught us very important things about the nature of language learning in both the blind and sighted child. One conclusion from these studies is that the meanings of individual words, contrary to the empiricist view, are not linked to combinations of sensory primitives, nor probably to higher-level primitives. For both nouns and verbs, certain aspects of their meanings are linked to syntax. For nouns, the distinction between count and mass nouns, or common and proper nouns is encoded in the syntax, and can be acquired through knowledge of language itself. For verbs, aspects of verb meaning such as the number and kind of arguments involved can also be acquired using evidence from the structure of language. If the meanings of words are not based on sensory or perceptual experience, then the blind child should be quite capable of acquiring meanings, whatever they might be.

A second conclusion is that the experience required for learning language is not what we might have thought it to be. If meanings are not based on visual experience, then the critical experience for learning a language is not embodied in the experience of seeing. That is, the deficit experienced by the blind child of not being able to see, may have considerably less to do with learning a language than one might have thought.

This is not to claim that the blind language learner is in all ways equivalent to the sighted. There clearly are pragmatic problems, such as information loss, that may force the blind learner and parent to seek alternative sources of information. For example, where visual sources of joint reference do not exist, alternatives must be sought. However, there is very little (if any) evidence that, under relatively normal conditions of development, language learning will be forever stalled for the blind child.

For researchers, this does not mean that the job is done. Quite the contrary – many aspects of the blind child's development are still not understood. In comparison to the sighted child, virtually nothing is known about the blind infant's knowledge of objects, space, and causality. Nor do we understand the ways in which the blind child and parent can establish and/or promote effective joint reference. We do not know what the effects are of continual and repeated failures to co-refer (either in the blind or sighted child), nor do we understand to what extent the blind child makes use of concrete reference in learning new words. In order to move forward on these and many other issues, it will be necessary to conduct well-designed and rigorous empirical studies that test critical questions without a priori biases about the true nature of knowledge.

Acknowledgement

The work reported in this chapter was supported by Social and Behavioral Sciences Research Grants #12-214 and 12-FY92-0493 from the March of Dimes Foundation and by NIH Grant #1-RO1-HD28675-01.

References

Andersen, E., Dunlea, A., and Kekelis, L. (1984). Blind children's language: resolving some differences. *Journal of Child Language, 11*, 645–664.

Baldwin, D. (1991). Infant contributions to the achievement of joint reference. *Child Development, 62*, 875–890.

Berkeley, G. (1709). An essay towards a new theory of vision. In D.M. Armstrong (Ed.), *Berkeley's Philosophical Writings*. New York: Macmillan, 1965.

Bigelow, A.E. (1984). The development of blind infants' search for dropped objects. Paper presented at International Conference on Infant Studies, New York.

Bloom, L. (1973). *One Word at a Time*. The Hague: Mouton.

Bloom, L., Lightbown, P., and Hood, L. (1975). Structure and variation in child language. *Monographs of the Society for Research in Child Development*, No. 160.

Bloom, P. (1996). Controversies in language acquisition: Word learning and the part of speech. In R. Gelman and T. Kit-Fong Au (Eds), *Perceptual and Cognitive Development*. San Diego: Academic Press.

Bruner, J.S. (1974/75). From communication to language: A psychological perspective. *Cognition, 3*, 255–287.

Butterworth, G. (1983). Structure of the mind in human infancy. In L. Lipsitt (Ed.), *Advances in Infancy Research*, Vol. 2. New Brunswick, N.J.: Ablex Corp.

Clark, E.V. (1973). What's in a word? On the child's acquisition of semantics in his first language. In T. Moore (Ed.), *Cognitive Development and the Acquisition of Language*. New York: Academic Press.

Collis, G.M. (1977). Visual coordination and maternal speech. In H.R. Schaffer (Ed.), *Studies in Mother–Infant Interaction*. London: Academic Press.

Dunlea, A. (1989). *Vision and the Emergence of Meaning: Blind and sighted children's early language*. Cambridge: Cambridge University Press.

Elman, J. (1993). Learning and development in neural networks: the importance of starting small. *Cognition, 48,* 71–99.

Fodor, J. (1981). *Representations.* Cambridge, MA: MIT Press.

Gelman, S. (1988). The development of induction within natural kind and artifact categories. *Cognitive Psychology, 20,* 65–95.

Gerken, L., Remez, R.E. and Landau, B. (1990). Function morphemes in young children's speech – perception and production. *Developmental Psychology, 26,* 204–216.

Gleitman, L.R. (1990). The structural sources of word meaning. *Language Acquisition,* 1, 3–55.

Grimshaw, J. (1981). Form, function, and the language acquisition device. In C.L. Baker and J. McCarthy (Eds), *The Logical Problem of Language Acquisition.* Cambridge, MA: MIT Press.

Hume, D. (1758). *An Inquiry Concerning Human Understanding.* Indianapolis, IN: Bobbs-Merrill, 1955.

Huttenlocher, J. (1974). The origins of language comprehension. In R.G. Solso (Ed.), *Theories of Cognitive Psychology.* Potomac, MD: Erlbaum.

Katz, N., Baker, E., and Macnamara, J. (1974). What's in a name? A study of how children learn common and proper names. *Child Development, 45,* 469–473.

Landau, B. and Gleitman, L.R. (1985). *Language and Experience: Evidence from the blind child.* Cambridge, MA: Harvard University Press.

Landau, B., Smith, L., and Jones, S. (1988). The importance of shape in early lexical learning. *Cognitive Development, 3,* 299–321.

Locke, J. (1690). *An Essay Concerning Human Understanding.* A.D. Woozley (Ed.). Cleveland: Meridian Books, 1964.

Mandler, J. (1992). How to build a baby: II. Conceptual primitives. *Psychological Review, 99,* 587–604.

Markman, E. (1989). *Categorization and Naming in Children: Problems of induction.* Cambridge, MA: MIT Press.

Markman, E. and Hutchinson, J. (1984). Children's sensitivity to constraints on word meaning: Taxonomic versus thematic relations. *Cognitive Psychology, 20,* 501–524.

Mills, A. E. (Ed.) (1983). *Language Acquisition in the Blind Child: Normal and deficient.* London: Croom Helm.

Pinker, S. (1989). *Learnability and Cognition.* Cambridge, MA: MIT Press.

Rescorla, L. (1980). Overextension in early language development. *Journal of Child Language, 7,* 321–335.

Waxman, S. (1994). The development of an appreciation of specific linkages between linguistic and conceptual organization. *Lingua, 92,* 229–257.

Chapter Three

Degrees of developmental and linguistic freedom

John L. Locke

Barbara Landau (Chapter 2) has proposed that developmental cognitive and linguistic scientists put aside their commonsense biases in order to pursue a research agenda that seriously addresses the role of vision in language learning. She suggests, for example, that we ask empirical questions about the types of lexical meaning cues that young blind children actually detect. When pondering the role of experience in language learning, she also invites us to think in very detailed, definitive ways about what experience means.

In the previous chapter Landau argues for the reasonableness of the possibility that linguistic development represents a collaboration. Infants hold their end up by bringing to the developmental table some helpful presumptions about the possible structure of linguistic systems. Her proposals are consistent with many of the emergent findings in the developmental cognitive and neurosciences, and well worth considering.

One of the great questions about our species' capability for linguistic communication is how it reaches full flower in the infant. This necessitates discovery of the elements on which language depends, and so it makes sense that we would want to estimate the relative contributions of genetics and environmental stimulation. Some theorists, like Pinker (1994), have argued that our young are preadapted for grammatical behaviour, and that very little stimulation is necessary to crank up this capacity. Others, like Snow (1995), have concentrated on the role of the environment, including the naturally didactic practices of mothers.

If the issue is what environments have to be like in order for our species' linguistic capability to develop, apparently the study of blind children is likely to be relatively uninformative. For no one seems to have evidence that blindness single-handedly blocks the development of grammatical capacity or the ability to exercise it. The grand biological issue is therefore moot, and we conclude that vision alone makes little, if any, contribution to the development of linguistic capacity.

But there are several reasons why blindness could still affect the development of language. First, consider children who experience delays in their language development, for whatever reason. If they are sighted, vision may offer these children compensatory possibilities that can be exploited naturally by the child or in programmes of clinical intervention. If the children are blind, the compensatory possibilities are accordingly diminished. In both cases the importance of vision may perceptibly wax as the efficiency of other systems wanes. Of course, children with multiple disabilities will usually be of less interest to the theorist than those with only one disability, but they exist, and therefore must concern all of us in some way.

The second contribution of vision to language relates to the rate or quality of blind children's language learning. Landau's research addresses these issues by asking situational questions about the specific functions that underlie the concept of experience. Some of the conclusions that Landau seeks to rebut were inherited from a previous generation of researchers, who did their research before the developmental neuro- and cognitive science revolutions were fully launched or able to report initial results. But now we have some new understandings about how the brain and mind develop. In the pages to follow, I will ask how these new understandings might influence underlying assumptions about the role of vision in the learning of language.

Brain development

When immature individuals are denied access to the amount and quality of sensory experience that is needed for development of experience-independent information storage systems of the brain, those systems are colonized or taken over by other information storage systems. For example, Neville and her colleagues (Neville, Schmidt and Kutas, 1983) have reported that individuals who are born deaf use areas of auditory cortex to process visual stimulation. This is a clear case of a developmental maxim: if it is not used for the purpose that nature intended, some other function will snatch it.

It might be assumed by analogy, although, to my knowledge, the relevant experiments have not been performed, that congenitally blind individuals use portions of their visual cortex to process sound. Many years ago, it was reported that congenitally blind adults are amazingly accurate at localizing sound sources, presumably better than sighted individuals (Kellogg, 1962). This puts a finer point on the lay assumption that people who lose a sense automatically compensate by developing other senses, and supplies a reason: their brains have more cells, and perhaps more elaborate information processing networks, dedicated to the task.

It seems likely that blind infants take in referential and affective information that, to the sighted person, is conveyed only by eye. If auditory localization is possible because sound reaches one ear slightly faster and louder than the other, it makes sense to ask if blind people are aware of the auditory equivalents of head movements and other activity that sighted people miss. When people look to one side or the other, they usually turn their head as well as their eyes, a manoeuvre that is not without acoustic consequences, and I would expect auditorily-compensated blind children to have a fairly good idea of where in space the speaker's topic might be located. Moreover, if a person said 'Look at that' while looking at a flying bird or a slithering snake, it would not be surprising if the listener could tell which animal it was from the acoustic product of an aimed vocal tract, a vocal tract that was elongated upwards or bent downwards, depending on which animal it was. These speculations can be confirmed by appropriate research, but the point is that, as Landau argues, blind children may have access to much of the same information as sighted children.

Modular cognitive operations

At one time, if facial imitation was observed in a one-year-old, it would have been claimed that this capacity was enabled by a previously acquired store of motor command and facial expression equivalences. It would have been argued that this set of equivalences was acquired through experience, perhaps when the infant looked at him or herself in a mirror while expressing a range of facial expressions, thereby discovering what happens to his or her own face when certain commands are sent, learning which commands produce which configurations of the eyes and mouth, and inferring which commands to send when seeking to reproduce the facial activity of others.

All this has changed. Recent experiments indicate that little or no sensory experience is needed for mental operations that in the past have logically seemed to require it. Meltzoff (1986) has demonstrated that 45-minutes-old neonates reproduce some facial gestures, even before they have seen an unmasked face or seen their own face in a mirror. The old, mirror-type explanations do not indicate how this happens. In all candour, developmental neuroscience has yet to come up with a better answer, one that responds to Studdert-Kennedy's (1991) eloquent question 'How does the light get into the muscle?' About all that can be said is that in evolutionary history, the light must have got into the muscles of our hominid ancestors.

Applied to spoken language, countless philosophers and psychologists have reasoned that it is in babbling that infants acquire articulatory maps that link speech-like movements and their usual auditory consequences. But in Kuhl and Meltzoff (1982), one notes that at four to five months of age, that is, prior to the usual babbling period, infants are already aware of which sounds go with spread lips and open mouths.

Ontogenetic tinkering

It is not strictly true that our young are allowed by their brains and bodies to do the things that they do. Young members of our adaptive species can, and frequently do, reach desired goals without having all the conventional hardware or experience. I like to show my students a film of a young man who was born without arms. In the film, he pours water from a jug by inserting his toes through the jug handle, transporting the jug to the recipient's glass, and tilting his foot to pour. He gave his brain the task of figuring out how to make the leg, ankle, and toes do this, and undoubtedly developed new brain structures in the process (for an illustration with string-playing musicians, see Elbert, Pantev, Wienbruch, Rockstroh and Taub, 1995).

Occasionally infants are born without a tongue or left cerebral hemisphere but are nonetheless able to speak. This never ceases to amaze observers, but the message from these accidents of nature is not that they leave the affected individuals with the ability to do everything the same way as the rest of us. Language is robust because it rests on a number of supporting systems and this polygenic property is also responsible for redundancies in the system. Extra parts may therefore be appropriated and slightly modified by individuals whose mental inheritance includes the ability to tinker up results.

Tinkering was selected for in evolutionary history and is with us today. It can be thought of as the source of what is called 'compensatory capacity'. It requires some potentially usable parts and a sense of the desired contemporaneous functions. Because of this ability to extend one's behavioural repertoire through tinkering, it is not illogical to say that vision makes a limited contribution to language in the blind and a large contribution to language in the sighted.

Language mechanisms are amodal

Although all of the world's 4000 to 6000 national languages are spoken, infants learn signed languages just as quickly as spoken ones (Meier and Newport, 1990) and later will use many of the same neural mechanisms in their processing (Haglund, Ojemann, Lettich, Bellugi and Corina, 1993). That they can learn with equal ease two such different systems should open our minds to the possibility that infants may also be able to learn one system in at least two broadly different ways.

The canalization for language involves a broad canal, allowing the child many degrees of freedom in negotiating a developmental growth path that will suit the particular circumstance of the language learner.

Linguistic communication is redundant

Linguistic communication is supported by a rich system of facial and vocal activities that convey affective, indexical, and referential information. These activities include eye movements, and changes in mouth configuration and head posture; variations in tone of voice; and interactions between facial and vocal activity with each other and the speaker's intended message. These displays collectively produce the effective message. It is particularly relevant to the present discussion that many of the indexical and affective messages conveyed by voice are also conveyed by face, and vice-versa. These redundant systems may involve some shared central and peripheral hardware, which would not be surprising inasmuch as their evolutionary histories are also intertwined (Andrew, 1963).

Take facial affect. In an experiment by Tartter (1980), speakers were instructed to read while either smiling or straightfaced. Naïve listeners associated smiled vocalizations with the act of smiling, or considered these utterances to be happier sounds, than unsmiled vocalizations. Acoustic analyses revealed that smiling raised the fundamental frequency and the first three formants (harmonics) in most of the speakers. In some of the speakers, amplitude and duration were also increased by smiling (Tartter and Braun, 1994).

Ohala (1983; 1984) has suggested that phylogeny could have given us the smile for acoustic reasons. Primate infants have short vocal tracts relative to adults and vocalize with higher formant frequencies. They are also relatively unthreatening. Using a physical model of the vocal tract, Ohala demonstrated that mouth-corner retraction, which is associated with smiling, shortens the tract. This should slightly raise the frequency of the first formant and the perceptible pitch of the speaker's voice.

Ohala has also suggested that lip retraction may have facilitated pitch elevation in animals that wished to appear submissive, pointing to observations that in non-human primates smiling and high-pitched vocalization co-occur. He speculated that in phylogeny, natural selection favoured animals that uttered high pitched vocalizations while retracting their lips (that is, smiling). Ultimately, these animals merely smiled when threatened by animals who also happened to respond sympathetically to infants in distress. In the course of time, according to Ohala, this behaviour became ritualized into social smiling.

There are other non-arbitrary relationships between sound and physical appearance. Morton (1977) has suggested a direct relationship between low frequency voice and the size of the animal producing a sound. One of his motivation structure rules thus holds that, 'The larger the animal, the lower the sound frequency it *can* produce'. If humans have such rules, the blind child probably could estimate an individual's size from vocal cues alone.

The point is that the voice is rich with information about who we are, how we feel, and what we might mean or intend to convey. This has been largely ignored by psychology and linguistics, giving rise to models of language processing that are invalid. But blind children *don't know from* language processing models, they only know what they know. I suspect this is a lot more than the rest of us think.

Meanings and units of meaning

It has become increasingly evident in recent years that children's meaningful utterances are heavily formulaic. Children frequently use phrases before the single words that, to the adult listener, are contained therein (Peters, 1983). They use words appropriately before they know what the words mean.

I think we have been kidding ourselves for a long time when we talk with pride about the generativity of language. Of course we can generate language, but that does not mean we do it every time we speak. Of course we can use language creatively, but many of our utterances are heavily reproductive. Tannen (1987) has written about the tendency, if not emotional need, of people to speak repetitively.

Much of our language is off the rack rather than custom-tailored, and it is highly figurative. There should therefore be little reason for surprise if we hear a blind person say 'I see what you mean' or even 'I saw Bob yesterday'. Most sighted people would not say 'I saw Bob yesterday' if they only talked to him on the telephone, or read his words on a computer screen. But when we do see Bob, and later say that we have done so, we do not imply that we had the visual experience of seeing Bob so much as that we were in the type of physical arrangement that permits visual experience. That we did also have that type of sensory experience will usually be irrelevant. I therefore see no reason why 'Trees are green' should automatically mean less to a blind child than 'Policemen are our friends' means to all children. To the infant, all words are lexical articles of faith, to be pronounced proudly and confidently.

Early experience tends to escape our notice

There are other types of experience besides those that have been considered the most relevant in a grammatical linguistic context. Some types of knowledge, such as which types of signals to pay the most attention to, are critical to the development of language. These may not be built-in, but it will certainly look that way because infants reveal these biases very early in postnatal life.

Neonatal humans pay attention to the voices of adult females and prefer their mother's voice to those of other women (DeCasper and Fifer, 1980). This is the result of previous experience. In ducklings, a preference for conspecific vocalization reflects prior exposure in the egg to the duckling's own vocalizations or conspecific vocalization (Gottlieb, 1991a; b). If there is a weak pre-adaptation for conspecific vocalization, it can be overridden by early exposure to heterospecific vocalization.

Sensory filters and attentional biases are not knowledge. They do participate in the acquisition of knowledge, but the infant still has to be motivated to engage in the activities that import information into the brain.

No one knows why the normally constituted human infant begins to talk. I have speculated elsewhere that infants possess a desire to be recognized as a person and to be conferred membership and status in a group. This adds to the infant's motivation to talk and do things that, as it so happens, advance linguistic and communicative development (Locke, 1996; in press). Infants with a central plan as to what the behaviour will need to be like, an endogenous drive to achieve certain goals, and the ability to appropriate existing parts will usually be able to make a go of it whether or not Nature provides all the orthodox tools. If blind infants' development of language is not terribly different quantitatively from that of sighted infants, does this mean that language requires no experience? We might just as well conclude that if a child with no tongue talks with some level of intelligibility then the tongue plays no role in speech.

Landau has asked two key questions. If given comparable non-visual information about focus of attention, can the blind child also take advantage of this information in word learning? In the normal course of early development, what is the likelihood that a blind infant's mother or father actually does provide comparable information about attentional focus? These questions are testable, in one form or another, and could tell us a great deal about the adaptations both of blind infants and their parents.

Landau doubts Dunlea's conclusion that the blind child's vocabulary differs from that of the sighted child to any appreciable degree. Her doubts seem justified. They bring to mind dozens of studies of the language of children with so-called specific language impairment (SLI). The phonology, morphology, syntax, and lexical development of these children have been repeatedly compared to those of younger, typically developing children. And, although there is evidence that many children with SLI have abnormal genetic histories and brains, there is no real evidence that they process or produce language differently than perfectly normal younger children (Locke, 1994).

Experience is a biological construct

From this discussion, it might appear that the environment plays no role in language development. Nothing could be further from the truth. The development of the child's linguistic capacity is a richly experiential enterprise, but the requisite experience is not opposed by factors that are innate or biological. To the contrary, the stimulation needed for language is provided indirectly by genetic material that was supplied by thousands of years of evolutionary history (Cosmides and Tooby, 1994).

The environment matters, but the mattering is difficult to witness. Under ordinary circumstances, it is harder to see how an unshared social environment affects language than it is to see how different rearing practices affect personality or intelligence (Plomin and Daniels, 1987). The reason, in part, is that linguistic stimulation is usually available to all infants in the basic amounts that are needed for development.

It is often said that language is robust because it takes so much to discourage its development. The function of language also has this characteristic, although this is less self-evident since there are so many different enabling systems operating during its development. These systems provide the infant who is missing something with degrees of developmental linguistic freedom.

References

Andrew, R. J. (1963). The origin and evolution of the calls and facial expressions of the primates. *Behaviour, 20*, 1–109,

Cosmides, L. and Tooby, J. (1994). Origins of domain specificity: the evolution of functional organization. In Hirschfeld, L. A. and Gelman, S. A. (Eds), *Mapping the Mind: Domain specificity in cognition and culture*. Cambridge: Cambridge University Press.

DeCasper, A. and Fifer, W. P. (1980). On human bonding: newborns prefer their mothers' voices. *Science, 208*, 1174–1176.

Elbert, T., Pantev, C., Wienbruch, C., Rockstroh, B. and Taub, E. (1995). Increased cortical representation of the fingers of the left hand in string players. *Science, 270*, 305–307.

Gottlieb, G. (1991a). Experiential canalization of behavioral development: theory. *Developmental Psychology, 27*, 4–13.

Gottlieb, G. (1991b). Experiential canalization of behavioral development: results. *Developmental Psychology, 27*, 35–39.

Haglund, M. M., Ojemann, G. A., Lettich, E., Bellugi, U. and Corina, D. (1993). Dissociation of cortical and single unit activity in spoken and signed languages. *Brain and Language, 44*, 19–27.

Kellogg, W. N. (1962). Sonar system of the blind. *Science, 137*, 399–404.

Kuhl, P. K. and Meltzoff, A. N. (1982). The bimodal perception of speech in infancy. *Science, 218*, 1138–1141.

Locke, J. L. (1994). Gradual emergence of developmental language disorders. *Journal of Speech and Hearing Research, 37*, 608–616.

Locke, J. L. (1996). Why do infants begin to talk? Language as an unintended consequence. *Journal of Child Language, 23*, 251–268.

Locke, J. L. (in press). Towards a biological science of language development. In Barrett, M. (Ed.), *The Development of Language*. London: UCL Press.

Meier, R. P. and Newport, E. L. (1990). Out of the hands of babes: on a possible sign advantage in language acquisition. *Language, 66*, 1–23.

Meltzoff, A. N. (1986). Imitation, intermodal representation, and the origins of mind. In Lindblom, B. and Zetterstrom, R. (Eds), *Precursors of Early Speech*. New York: Stockton Press.

Morton, E. S. (1977). On the occurrence and significance of motivation-structural rules in some bird and mammal sounds. *American Naturalist, 111*, 855–869.

Neville, H. J., Schmidt, A. and Kutas, M. (1983). Altered visual-evoked potentials in congenitally deaf adults. *Brain Research, 266*, 127–132.

Ohala, J. J. (1983). Cross-language use of pitch: an ethological view. *Phonetica, 40*, 1–18.

Ohala, J. J. (1984). An ethological perspective on common cross-language utilization of F_0 of voice. *Phonetica, 41*, 1–16.

Peters, A. M. (1983). *The Units of Language Acquisition*. New York: Cambridge University Press.

Pinker, S. (1994). *The Language Instinct: The new science of language and mind*. London: Penguin Books.

Plomin, R. and Daniels, D. (1987). Why are children in the same family so different from one another? *Behavioral and Brain Sciences, 10*, 1–60.

Snow, C. (1995). Issues in the study of input: fine-tuning, universality, individual and developmental differences, and necessary causes. In MacWhinney, B. and Fletcher, P. (Eds), *NETwerken: bijdragen van het viffde NET symposium*. Antwerp Papers in Linguistics, 74: University of Antwerp.

Studdert-Kennedy, M. (1991). Language development from an evolutionary perspective. In Krasnegor, N., Rumbaugh, D., Schiefelbusch, R. and Studdert-Kennedy, M. (Eds), *Biological and Behavioral Determinants of Language Development*. Hillsdale, NJ: Erlbaum.

Tannen, D. (1987). Repetition in conversation: towards a poetics of talk. *Language, 63*, 574–605.

Tartter, V. C. (1980). Happy talk: perceptual and acoustic effects of smiling on speech. *Perception and Psychophysics, 27*, 24–27.

Tartter, V. C. and Braun, D. (1994). Hearing smiles and frowns in normal and whisper registers. *Journal of the Acoustical Society of America, 96*, 2101–2107.

Chapter Four

Reading without vision

Susanna Millar

Braille is the main system of written communication used by blind people throughout the world. It was originated by a blind person, Louis Braille (1809–1852), who was dissatisfied with the method of tactual reading by which he was taught as a child, and the system is still being monitored by people who are themselves experienced braillists. It is therefore clearly a useful system for blind people. The fact that it is more difficult to learn and is often read more slowly than print (although it can also produce fluent reading), makes it all the more important to find out how processing takes place.

Moreover, understanding how braille is learned and read raises a number of issues that depend directly on our understanding of the relation between what are usually called low level perceptual processes and so-called higher order linguistic and cognitive processes. The study of braille contributes to that understanding because it both resembles, and differs from, print in a number of ways. English braille is linguistically (in phonology, word meaning, semantics and syntax) identical with print. But it differs from print in three important respects: the physical format; the intake of information; and some aspects of orthography.

With regard to the physical format, all braille characters derive from one very small (6.2 mm high) matrix of 6 (2 × 3) raised dots. The characters have few distinguishing features, because the presence or absence of any dot denotes a different character. Both the small size and the absence of redundant features have important implications for learning to read.

The intake of information also differs from vision. In touch, information in reading for meaning is taken in during scanning rather than during the time a single pattern is being fixated, or touched without moving. The reverse is the case in visual reading, in which the intake of information occurs during fixations, not during saccades. In touch without vision, the organization of hand movements is crucial for keeping to the line, for keeping place in regressions, and for the transition from one line to the next when reading texts.

Orthography in braille is mainly based on the same, very imperfectly alphabetic system, as print. But in addition to regular alphabetically-defined phonemes for letters, and the same categories of irregular and exception words as print, English (Grade 2) braille also contains contracted forms. Some of these are single characters, or single characters prefaced by one to three dots, which represent whole words if they stand alone, flanked by spaces. The presence of these contracted forms means that braille also contains logographic forms. That is extremely important in principle, though we have far too little evidence as yet on how they are processed. Some findings that have a bearing on how they are coded will be considered later. These and other contractions which represent syllables, including syntactic markers, also have to be used within words in which the relevant letter clusters occur. There are a large number of rules which govern when and how contractions are to be used within words which have to be learned and used in reading and writing braille, in addition to the rules and/or conventions that govern English spelling. However, these problems will not be addressed in this chapter.

These three aspects of braille, namely the physical format, the intake of information, and orthography, will be considered in turn, mainly in terms of the author's own findings. The studies to which the chapter refers centre on the question of how people code braille inputs, and whether, and how, this changes with proficiency and experience in the acquisition and development of reading, in a system that differs from print in physical features, in modality and in some aspects of orthography.

The children who took part in the studies that will be mentioned were mainly congenitally, totally or near totally blind, but did not have known brain damage or deafness. Data on children with serious learning or reading disabilities are not included. Some of the later studies described also included several blind young people with minimal vision who had learned braille from the start. Brief mention will also be made of reading by adults who had learned braille relatively late in life. However, it is not possible to embark on the important issues raised by the presence of residual sight, and by prior experience of print reading.

The main focus here is on information processing in learning and reading braille by touch, rather than on blind children as a group. In the words of one headmaster, himself blind, 'There is nothing wrong with the blind except that they cannot see'. But two points are relevant to the general informational conditions that have to be taken into account both theoretically and in practice. First, the younger children are, the less they know, and the less familiar they are with all aspects of any situation. This means that they need more redundancy in information from all sources. Second, total absence of a sensory source, temporarily or permanently, produces not only a reduction in the information specific to that sense, it also reduces the partial overlap of that input with information from other sensory sources. Every modality contributes to the balance of multi-sensory and intersensory processes on which spatial coding depends. The total absence of vision mainly reduces current external reference cues and the overlap of that information with reference cues from other sources that normally complement and converge with these. It is important to identify precisely what inputs specific task and stimulus conditions afford in order to restore the reduction in (apparently) redundant, as well as in the specialized, information.

General theoretical frame

Theories of print reading are usually divided into bottom-up, top-down and interactive (for example, Rayner and Pollatsek, 1989), according to whether information is supposed to pass from the periphery to the centre, or is guided mainly by cognitive skills, or whether some interplay between perceptual and cognitive effects is assumed. Theories of braille reading have generally followed theories of print reading. Whole word methods were at one time advocated in braille (see Burklen, 1932) as well as in print. However, that is probably not the best means for learning braille (Millar, 1984; Nolan and Kederis, 1969). In practice, phonic (grapheme-phoneme recoding) methods are used far more in teaching braille.

The most influential theory for braille has been that reading is a data-driven, letter-by-letter process (Daneman, 1988; Nolan and Kederis, 1969; Foulke, 1982) which is based on the global shape of letters (Nolan and Kederis, 1969). The implication is that letter-by-letter reading remains the basis of processing also in fluent reading. The theory is a useful starting point, and will be used as such. But it does not account adequately for all the findings, and the differences are important in practice.

The general theoretical frame that I have used in my studies belongs to the broad class of interactive models. It is an extension of the view described previously to account for the evidence on spatial processing in blind conditions (Millar, 1981; 1994). It assumes that human information processing depends on convergent processing in active interrelated networks. Intersensory processing, including information from touch, movement and posture, converges and partly overlaps. The redundancy resulting from intersensory information is important in the spatial organization of inputs, and particularly so for inputs from the small, non-redundant braille patterns that afford few, if any, automatic reference cues.

The model proposed for braille reading assumes further convergence of the current activation of these connections with networks that represent previous verbal (phonological, lexical and semantic/syntactic) information. New input patterns activate and change, and are also changed by previous patterns of connections. The assumed interactions do not merely concern the direction (up or down) of the flow of information. The picture is rather of patterns of converging networks that produce informational redundancies as well as divergence in activation.

Overlap and redundancy in information are particularly important for young children, and even more so for blind children learning braille, because braille requires the association between networks that are inherently dedicated to processing information from different sources: hearing and speech for the language components, and touch and movement for the spatial and perceptual aspects respectively. It should be noted in passing that such specialization does not require the notion of strict modularity (Fodor, 1983) in the sense of isolated expert systems during normal development. Moreover, informational redundancy does not result simply from repeating the same information. Uncertainty is reduced (confidence is increased) by the convergence of complementary information from different sources (Millar, 1981).

The proposed model for braille reading is described in more detail elsewhere (Millar, 1997). The main point to be stressed here is the importance of providing redundant (overlap with familiar) information for young children, and particularly for young children learning and remembering braille, because braille learning involves active spatial organization of touch and movement inputs, the retrieval of verbal information, and the forming of new associations between sparse new haptic inputs and new phonological (for example, phonemic) and orthographic (spelling and contraction) input patterns. This point will be considered later.

The format of braille letters: tactual and phonological coding

To understand braille learning it is necessary to know precisely what information braille patterns afford and how that information is coded. Visually, individual braille characters look like quite *good* shapes, in the Gestalt sense of good form. The letter-by-letter theory of braille reading assumes that braille letter patterns are also recognized as global outline shapes by touch and that processing is based on these shapes. However, it was clear from cross-modal studies that recognition, even of three-dimensional shapes, is much poorer by touch than by vision (for example, Goodnow, 1971; Millar, 1971). Such findings raised the question of how braille patterns are coded, and whether tactual coding occurs at all in short-term memory. If so, it was also important to find out how coding by touch relates to recoding the patterns phonologically (Millar, 1975).

The importance of phonological coding for tasks involving short-term memory in development was not in doubt (for example, Conrad, 1964; 1971). For blind children, coding by sound is, of course, particularly important, in any case. The initial concern was rather whether tactual inputs could be coded at all in memory prior to naming.

Millar (1975) showed that the *feel* of raised dot patterns can indeed be coded in the short-term, but differs from phonological recoding and produces very small recall spans (at best 2–3 items). The study adapted the method pioneered by Conrad (1964; 1971), which demonstrated that children's short-term memory span increases with increased phonological recoding. In order to study coding by touch, the study used serial lists of braille letters that were tactually similar, as well as lists of letters that had phonologically similar names. Both lists were compared with lists of serial items that differed both tactually and in name sound. As in the study by Conrad (1971), progressively larger effects of phonological similarity were found to be associated with larger recall spans. The effects of tactual similarity, by contrast, had the opposite effect on recall spans. The finding was confirmed in a further study (Millar, 1978), which showed that the same participants who achieved immediate recall spans of about six letters that they could name, only obtained 2–3 item spans for tactual patterns that they could not name. This study also showed that the small size of span was due to tactual coding rather than to age or individual differences.

The small size of tactual recall spans prior to naming is, of course, of interest for teaching. The speed of letter naming on pre-test was associated with the recall span which children achieved subsequently when items were presented to touch. The findings suggest strongly that naming facility, or familiarity with the name-sound of letters, is a basic factor in larger span sizes. The pre-test was administered routinely at the time. But the relation of naming speed to phonological recoding and span size suggests that speed of retrieving familiar names from longer term memory is involved. Word familiarity effects have since been found to reduce age differences in the size of auditory spans (Henry and Millar, 1991). The findings are also consistent with other evidence which shows the involvement of longer-term memory in span size (for example, Hulme, Maughan, and Brown 1991; Watkins, 1977).

It was thus clear that, once beginning braillists have learned the name sounds for braille letters sufficiently well, they can use these to recode the tactual inputs phonemically. However, it was not initially obvious why tactually coded *feels* were so difficult to remember if they were indeed coded in terms of global letter shapes.

People have usually considered the small size of braille as the main problem, on the grounds that tactual acuity is poor. Anyone who feels a braille shape for the first time, without having seen it first, finds it extremely difficult to indicate the global shape of the pattern. Clarity of discrimination is indeed involved. But if initial tactual acuity were taken to indicate an actual limit on discriminative accuracy, it would be difficult to explain why fluent braillists have no problem in recognizing braille patterns, or how experience with braille could improve detection.

It seemed possible that poor recall could be due to poorly organized coding. The paradigm pioneered by Posner was adapted in further studies to test this possibility. Posner and Mitchell (1967) asked participants to match upper and lower case print letters to see whether the shape of letters made a difference even if they had the same name. English braille does not have capitals. Instead, the formats of letter pairs were altered by changing the size of the raised dots and the gaps between the dots in the braille letter patterns. Identical letter pairs took longer if they differed in format, even though the letter shapes as well as the letter names were identical. The hypothesis that braille patterns are not initially coded as global shapes, and that initial perception is based on dot density cues, was confirmed by a large number of studies using a variety of methods (see Millar, 1997). In summary, these studies showed that: beginning readers had to be trained to recognize the same shapes in enlarged (that is, *clearer*) form; outline (raised) shapes did not facilitate the recognition of the relevant dot patterns; left hand/right hemisphere advantages were not consistent over people, or studies, or tasks; naïve (sighted) participants failed to draw the shapes that they had learned to discriminate; young braillists did not draw letter shapes accurately even if they could name them; dot density cues, rather than shape symmetry, facilitated discrimination of patterns based on five and eight dot matrices; dot density rather than spatial (location) differences produced better performance with braille patterns.

Further studies also showed that perception of the patterns becomes spatially anchored and organized with training and experience. Several types of training methods are in fact routinely used by braille teachers for precisely this purpose. One method involves associating dot positions in the braille cell with numbers (1 2 3 × 4 5 6), and with the finger positions that produce the characters in writing with the Perkins braille machine. The mediation is by verbal (number) sequences. Another method is to encourage systematic exploration either with conventional or with enlarged forms. The mediation here is through systematic movements. These can be achieved by giving beginners advance information about the shapes, practice in scanning and by encouraging the spatial organization of movement patterns. Systematic exploration is based on constructive spatial (directional) organization of scanning movements and procedural knowledge of the shapes. A third method relies on passive touch by the fingertip. In principle, the top and sides of the fingerpad could be used as a spatial frame to which the location of dots in a cell can be related, although touch has to be momentary to prevent loss of sensation. A further method used in teaching braille is to encourage spatially organized (relative to the body) lateral scanning of lines of familiar words or short sentences.

The difficulty of coding braille patterns as global shapes is due to the physical composition of braille patterns in tactual conditions: the lack of salient features that could provide object-centred spatial anchors; the small size which makes it difficult to determine the position of dots by reference to ego-centric frames (for example, body midline), and the absence of concomitant external (surrounding) reference frame cues, which have to be sought or constructed through the use of hand movements when vision is excluded.

The evidence does *not* imply that shape coding by touch does not occur, let alone that it is impossible for blind children. The point is rather that shape coding is not automatic for braille patterns in touch, because the lack of salient features and small size of the patterns reduce the possibility of using any of the three forms of spatial coding initially to determine dot locations. In fact, the findings are quite consistent with evidence that the most common errors children make are dot omissions, confusions between letters with equal dot densities, and in letters that consist of more rather than fewer dots. Moreover, the methods used in practice to assist character identification by young children do indeed imply that the identification of braille characters requires assisted learning. Moreover, some top-down (verbal and spatial) processing is involved from the start in the assisted learning that has been mentioned. As most braille teachers are aware, it is worthwhile paying attention to the specific spatial frames that particular methods imply.

The intake of information and scanning movements

The fact that movement as well as touch is involved in what is normally called touch or haptics is, of course, well known. More important, however, is the fact that the intake of information in reading by touch actually depends on intersensory processes. Inputs from touch, from movements and posture cues converge and require spatial organization. That is even more relevant in reading for meaning, which is the main object of reading, than in the recognition of single characters, important though such recognition is. The intake of information in reading connected prose depends crucially on the organization of movements for the spatial as well as for the verbal tasks that are involved in reading texts by touch.

The important question is what function the movements of the two hands actually have. The role of hand movements in establishing spatial references, as well as processing the verbal information, can be observed by watching the reading fingers move over braille texts from below transparent surfaces (Millar, 1988). For instance, observations of the finger movements of a bright seven year old who was reading a story silently showed that two-handed reading may actually involve a complete dissociation between using the hand to take in verbal information, and using the hand as a spatial guide. It was clear that this bright little seven year old was actually using only her left hand to read. The posture of the right hand showed that it was used as a guide. The thumb and forefinger were pressed together, thus forming a ridge which was passed along the braille line. By contrast, another very bright, slightly younger girl had not as yet perfected the guiding and place-keeping dissociation between the two hands. She was reading aloud extremely well, but stopped when she realized that the sentence no longer made sense, and returned to the beginning of the line where she found the word that she had left out. In other words, she showed a very intelligent use of the semantic context to repair her as yet imperfect mastery of the spatial lay-out. The use of semantic context is often considered an inferior strategy that ought to be discouraged. However, in this instance at least, it seemed to have provided important feedback about a spatial error to the child.

Using the two hands systematically for keeping to the line, and providing a spatial anchor to keep the place while the other hand moves to the next line, is often quite difficult for beginning young readers. Effects of prior experience and teaching also show up in types of scanning. An elderly lady who had learned braille for only a year but was formerly a fluent print reader, was observed to use consistent circular movements over each letter shape. Such movements were much more streamlined in another former print reader who had more experience of braille.

The most elegant fluent readers can be found among adolescent students who have learned braille from the start. The two hands take over from each other at about the middle of the line. The right hand reads while the left proceeds to the beginning of the next line, and the left starts reading the new line as soon as the right hand has finished the last line or is in transit to joint the left hand. Most fluent readers also make sure that they know the relative extent and spatial layout of the text by rapid hand movements over the sheet prior to reading. Moreover, reading becomes faster later in the text than initially, showing the progressive use of construing the gist. It is clear that the hand movements at that level of proficiency are driven by both the spatial and verbal demands of the task.

The alternate intake of verbal and spatial information during scanning by the two hands has also been demonstrated by the latency data from video recording the fingers with simultaneous cumulative (1/100 sec) timing (Millar, 1987a). The video frame times are transcribed for each hand separately by observers who do not know braille. Evidence from mean frame times for the text locations touched by the right and left fingers of ten proficient readers showed that the two hands are used alternately for processing verbal and spatial aspects of the text. The findings suggested parallel processing of information from different domains (spatial and verbal), but not from within the same domain (that is, verbal decoding).

Finally, the type and speed of finger movements have also shown that the actual pick-up of perceptual information differs with proficiency and, perhaps more startling, with the type of verbal processing that the task demands (Millar, 1987b). The study used texts that were rotated by 90 degrees and hand positions that were either inverted similarly, or remained in the same position as in normal reading. Both rotated texts were, of course, more difficult, and so slowed reading. The important point, however, was to test what perceptual features were being picked up. If subjects were coding shapes, however fast, the actual position of the fingers should not have had any effect. The alternative possibility, originally suggested by Grunewald (1966), was that fluent reading depends on *dynamic* or temporally extended flow patterns in lateral scanning. If so, leaving the hand in the normal position in scanning a rotated text should disrupt the normal lateral shear pattern on the ball of the scanning finger. By contrast, inverting the scanning finger would preserve lateral shear patterns, even though the inverted movement was more awkward. Two tasks were used: reading connected texts for meaning and searching for a letter in the texts. The results showed that the task made all the difference for proficient readers. For slow readers neither task nor finger positions made any difference. But for proficient readers, reading for meaning was totally disrupted by disrupting lateral scanning. In the letter search task, the finger position made little difference, because the participants used circular movements, suggesting that they were processing shapes.

The findings thus showed that the pick-up of perceptual information changes with the reading task in a manner that depends on proficiency. Proficient readers use dynamic lateral scanning that produced shear (temporally organized dot-gap density) patterns on the ball of the finger in reading for comprehension; but circular (shape) movements in letter search. A further study with a different method further confirmed these findings (Millar, 1987b, experiment 2).

Taken together, the findings suggest that the relations between the verbal and spatial aspects of reading cannot be fitted into any model that assumes purely data-driven (letter-by-letter) processing. The influence of task effects was marked. However these effects occurred primarily in proficient reading, suggesting that there are changes with proficiency in the interactions between cognitive influences and what are normally considered low level perceptual processes. The progressive organization and differentiation of hand movements for verbal and spatial aspects of the reading task have a number of practical implications. These suggest that assisted learning needs to be flexible rather than adhering rigidly to a single method. But such implications have yet to be tested in the field.

Aspects of orthography: effects of proficiency, tasks and contracted forms

It is of some practical importance to note that levels of proficiency in reading, as well as the conditions and demands of different types of reading task, affect phonological coding processes. Moreover, phonological coding is not all of the same kind. For instance, although the letter-by-letter theory could not explain all the findings adequately, there is evidence that beginning braille readers and slow braille readers do rely on letter-by-letter reading in the sense of an assembled phonology which involves coding (alphabetically defined) phonemes. A series of studies used Baddeley's method of articulatory suppression (see Baddeley, 1986) The method prevents subvocal speech by having subjects pronounce a meaningless syllable (such as 'blah') repeatedly while reading silently. Some young beginning braille readers were quite incapable of making out any letters in these conditions, while proficient readers showed no effect when reading easy stories. With difficult texts their comprehension was impaired but speed was not affected, suggesting interference with memory and the integration of words into gist, rather than interference with phonemic recoding (Millar, 1990), similar to findings with visual texts (Baddeley, 1986; Hardyk and Petrinovitch, 1970).

However, there is evidence that young children also code words by sound to sustain memory in difficult or ambiguous conditions. The studies which showed this used pairs of single character contracted words (some prefaced by one dot) and legally contracted or less contracted homophone words to test for effects of word length and phonological coding in sentence judgements. Using single character contracted words (for example, WHICH) and less contracted homophones (for example, witCH) has several advantages. Both are legal words so there is no need to create nonword (nonsense) homophones that could produce confusions, because children rightly expect the words they read to have meaning. Contracted and less contracted homophone words also differ maximally in graphemic form and word length without differing in word frequency. Moreover, phonological effects produced by single character words, or by single characters preceded by a dot, cannot be due to the serial grapheme-phoneme recoding and blending that is characteristic of assembled phonology.

The results showed that young, less proficient, readers made differentially more phonological errors in sentences with sound/sense ambiguities than more proficient readers. Thus, less proficient readers accepted sentences that sounded correct but would make no sense if they had coded the meaning of the word. Moreover, less proficient readers also showed word length effects in their latencies. They took more time (first pass) to scan the longer than the shorter words, but made the same error on both. They must, therefore, have coded the word sounds of contracted (logograph) words, which could not have been recoded phonemically, as well as the more fully spelt out words which could have been recoded character-by-character. The homophone errors by beginners are similar to findings on regular print nonwords (Coltheart, Laxon, Rickard, and Eldon, 1988). But the findings for contracted homophones in braille show that phonological errors cannot be attributed solely to grapheme-phoneme coding or to assembled phonology. Word length had no significant effect on latencies of proficient readers.

All readers, including beginners, took longer over the same target words when these were in the wrong context. This suggested that, though beginners relied on phonological coding of the ambiguous (sound/sense) words, even they had some inkling of the fact that the meanings of the target words did not quite fit the sense of the sentences. However, unlike the proficient readers who reprocessed the ambiguous words, as shown by regression times, beginners failed to check on the meaning of words that sounded correct. The reason for such failures to check are not entirely clear. It may be that their greater reliance on coding by sound was simply due to an effect of greater memory load for the younger children. However, lexical checking may be particularly important for young blind children who necessarily have to rely on sounds to a greater extent. Whichever it is, the issue clearly has to be taken seriously.

Finally, I want to turn briefly to a third type of phonological coding, namely the coding of words in terms of syllables. There is a general consensus that syllables are important in speech perception (see, for example, Liberman, Shankweiler, Liberman, Fowler and Fischer, 1977; Rayner and Pollatsek, 1989; Van Orden, Pennington and Stone, 1990), and are detected by young children more easily than phonemes (for example, Gleitman and Rozin, 1973). But it has also been argued that syllables are central to silent reading for meaning (see Spoehr and Smith, 1975; Rayner and Pollatsek, 1989), although this assumption is controversial (for example, Kliegl, Olson and Davidson, 1983). The point is potentially important for the use of contracted forms in braille.

It was important to test the use of syllables first in normal silent reading of a connected text on normally spelt (legally mainly uncontracted) words. The aim was to compare the effect of length in syllables with the effect of length in letters for groups of words that were matched on average word frequency, so as not to confound word length and frequency (for example, Zipf, 1935). Unlike the sentence judgements in which the homophone words were crucial to judging the sense of sentences, no special attention was drawn to the target words, and these words were not crucial to the gist of the story. The upshot was that word length in letters had large effects on scanning (first pass) latencies in all readers. By contrast, there was only a very marginal effect of word length in syllables even for slow readers, and no effect at all of word length in syllables for proficient readers. The implications for contracted words have since also been tested more directly. Syllables, as such, unless they carry meaning, do not seem to be central in proficient silent braille reading. The frequency of contractions is probably more important (for example, Lorimer, Tobin, Gill and Douce, 1982). Certainly, familiarity with particular forms, for instance by experienced braillists compared to the long-standing ortho-graphic/phonological habits of former print readers, again seems to be the most powerful factor (Millar, 1995).

But the point to which I want to draw attention in considering the results of these studies is the very different effect on processing by proficient and less proficient readers when the target words were crucial to the task, compared to effects on target words that did not have to be remembered. The influence that task conditions have on processing has important implications both for evaluating children's performance, but also for understanding the differences in processing that apparently small differences in information can produce.

Some implications

It was suggested at the beginning of this chapter that the picture of a data-driven hierarchical process from letter shapes to verbal compre-hension with some top-down effects is not an adequate account of how braille reading takes place.

The findings which were reviewed briefly in this chapter fall into three broad categories. First, perception of braille patterns is not initially based on spatially organized shapes. Relatively unsystematic movements pro-duce dot-density disparities that are coded in memory but produce small recall spans. Higher order phonological, lexical and semantic processes are involved in the learning process from the start, and they are influ-enced, in turn, by the available perceptual information. Second, hand movements are progressively organized to gain spatial reference cues as well as verbal information. The two forms of information are used recip-rocally during reading acquisition. For instance, semantic coherence is often lost before children have established adequate place-keeping strategies. But semantic cues also provide feedback about the loss of spatial reference and consequent repairs. Third, the changes that take place with proficiency cannot be explained by a single factor, nor do they suggest permanent changes in types of coding. Instead, there seems to be a progressive organization and streamlining of the connections between all the subsidiary spatial and verbal skills and their relation to task effects. Perceptual skills are not simply a limiting static factor. The perceptual pick-up becomes progressively differentiated, so that the perceptual cues that are processed in lateral scans in reading for meaning differ from the spatial features picked up in letter search.

The theoretical frame of interactive processing and progressive convergence and organization of connections between current and stored intersensory (movement and touch) and verbal (phonological, lexical, semantic and orthographic) information provides an explanatory frame for the evidence on how braille reading takes place. The hypothesis that more redundancy and overlap of information from different sources (familiarity, repetition and support from converging inputs) is needed earlier in development explains many of the differences between beginning and proficient readers.

The practical implications are not that one method of teaching is superior to all others. Different forms of coding seem to be needed for different types of reading tasks. The main problem is rather how to provide sufficient redundancy of information without overloading the system. If there is one research project that I would urge for the future it is to look at the conditions under which redundant information from different sources facilitates rather than interferes with learning and recall.

References

Baddeley, A. D. (1986). *Working Memory.* Oxford: The Clarendon Press.

Burklen, K. (1932). *Touch Reading of the Blind* (trans. F. K. Merry). New York: American Foundation for the Blind.

Coltheart, V., Laxon, V., Rickard, M. and Eldon, C. (1988). Phonological recoding in reading for meaning by adults and children. *Journal of Experimental Psychology: Learning, Memory and Cognition, 14,* 387–397.

Conrad, R. (1964). Acoustic confusions in immediate memory. *British Journal of Psychology, 55,* 75–84.

Conrad, R. (1971). The chronology of the development of covert speech in children. *Developmental Psychology, 5,* 398–405.

Daneman, M. (1988). How reading braille is both like and unlike reading print. *Memory and Cognition, 16,* 497–504.

Fodor, J. (1983). *The Modularity of Mind: An Essay on Faculty Psychology.* Cambridge: Cambridge University Press.

Foulke, E. (1982). Reading braille. In W. Schiff and E. Foulke (Eds), *Tactual Perception: A source book.* New York: Cambridge University Press.

Gleitman, L. R. and Rozin, P. (1973). Teaching by use of a syllabary. *Reading Research Quarterly, 8,* 447–483.

Goodnow, J. J. (1971). Eye and hand: differential memory and its effects on matching. *Neuropsychologia, 42*, 1187–1201.

Grunewald, A. P. (1966). A braille reading machine. *Science, 154*, 144–146.

Hardyk, C. D. and Petrinovitch, L. R. (1970). Subvocal speech and comprehension level as a function of the difficulty level of the reading material. *Journal of Verbal Learning and Verbal Behaviour, 9*, 647–652.

Henry, L. and Millar, S. (1991). Memory span increase with age: A test of two hypotheses. *Journal of Experimental Child Psychology, 51*, 459–484.

Hulme, C., Maughan, S. and Brown, G. D. A. (1991). Memory for familiar and unfamiliar words: Evidence for a long-term memory contribution to short-term memory span. *Journal of Memory and Language, 30*, 685–701.

Liberman, I. Y., Shankweiler, D., Liberman, A.M., Fowler, C. and Fischer, F. W. (1977). Phonetic segmentation and recoding in the beginning reader. In A. S. Reber and D. L. Scarborough (Eds), *Towards a Psychology of Reading.* New York: John Wiley.

Lorimer, J., Tobin, M. J., Gill, J. and Douce, J. L. (1982). *A Study of Braille Contractions.* Birmingham: Royal National Institute for the Blind.

Kliegl, R., Olson, K. R. and Davidson, B. J. (1983). On problems of unconfounding perceptual and language processes. In K. Rayner (Ed.), *Eye Movements in Reading: Perceptual and language processes.* New York: Academic Press.

Millar, S. (1971). Visual and haptic cue utilization by preschool children: The recognition of visual and haptic stimuli presented separately and together. *Journal of Experimental Child Psychology, 12*, 88–94.

Millar, S. (1975). Effects of tactual and phonological similarity on the recall of Braille letters by blind children. *British Journal of Psychology, 66*, 193–201.

Millar, S. (1978). Short-term serial tactual recall: Effects of grouping tactually probed recall of braille letters and nonsense shapes by blind children. *British Journal of Psychology, 68*, 17–24.

Millar, S. (1981). Crossmodal and intersensory perception and the blind. In R. D. Walk and H. L. Pick, Jr (Eds), *Intersensory Perception and Sensory Integration.* New York: Plenum Press.

Millar, S. (1984). Strategy choices by young braille readers. *Perception, 13*, 567–579.

Millar, S. (1987a). The perceptual *window* in two-handed braille. Do the left and right hands process text simultaneously? *Cortex, 23*, 111–222.

Millar, S. (1987b). Perceptual and task factors in fluent braille. *Perception, 16*, 521–536.

Millar, S. (1988). An apparatus for recording hand movements. *British Journal of Visual Impairment and Blindness, 6*, 87–90.

Millar, S. (1990). Articulatory coding in prose reading: Evidence from braille on changes with skill. *British Journal of Psychology, 18*, 205–219.

Millar, S. (1994). *Understanding and Representing Space: Theory and evidence from studies with blind and sighted children.* Oxford: Clarendon Press.

Millar, S. (1995). Sound, sense, syllables and sense in prose reading by touch. Paper presented at the Birmingham Scientific Meeting of the Experimental Psychology Society, July 12th.

Millar, S. (1997). *Reading by Touch*. London: Routledge.

Nolan, C. Y. and Kederis, C. J. (1969). *Perceptual Factors in Braille Word Recognition*. New York: American Foundation for the Blind.

Posner, M. I. and Mitchell, R. F. (1967). Chromatic analysis of classification. *Psychological Review, 74*, 392–409.

Rayner, K. and Pollatsek, A. (1989). *The Psychology of Reading*. Englewood Cliffs, New Jersey: Prentice Hall.

Spoehr, K. T. and Smith, E. E. (1975). The role of orthographic and phonotactic rules in perceiving letter patterns. *Journal of Experimental Psychology: Human Perception and Performance, 1*, 21–34.

Van Orden, G., Pennington B. and Stone, G. O. (1990). Word identification in reading and the promise of subsymbolic linguistics. *Psychological Review, 97*, 488–522.

Watkins, M. J. (1977). The intricacy of the memory span. *Memory and Cognition, 5*, 529–534.

Zipf, G. F. (1935). *The Psychobiology of Language: An introduction to dynamic philology*. New York: Houghton Mifflin.

Chapter Five

Learning to read in blind and sighted children

Margaret Harris
and
Fiona Barlow-Brown

In this chapter we shall consider how the way that blind children learn to read braille compares with the way that sighted children learn to read print. Much of the chapter will be concerned with the initial stages of learning to read, which is where the greatest differences between blind and sighted children are evident.

We begin by reviewing studies of early print reading where we highlight factors that predict reading success and, in particular, we discuss the importance of letter knowledge. Then we compare the acquisition of such knowledge via print and via braille and discuss some of the special problems that confront blind children when they first begin learning to read. In the next section, we consider how blind and sighted children develop reading strategies and pinpoint some differences between the two groups. Then we consider how braille reading and text reading might differ as children become fluent readers. We also consider how teaching strategies influence children's learning of braille. In a final section, we explore ways in which the reading and pre-reading experiences of young braille learners might be enhanced.

Beginning to read in print

In the last decade or so a great deal of the research into learning to read has been devoted to an exploration of the various factors that contribute to early reading success among sighted children. Much of the agenda for recent research was set by two pioneering studies carried out by Lundberg and his colleagues in Scandinavia (Lundberg, Olofsson and Wall, 1980) and by Bradley and Bryant (1983) in the UK. Both research programmes highlighted children's phonological knowledge as an important contributor to reading success.

Phonological awareness

Lundberg *et al.* (1980) trained pre-school children in Sweden on a wide range of tasks involving phonological knowledge. These included recognition of rhymes, finding the initial phoneme in a word and segmenting a word into its constituent syllables. Lundberg *et al.* found that children who were trained in these tasks made better reading progress than comparable children who had not received this training.

Bradley and Bryant (1983) also carried out a training study. They presented pre-school children with one of three types of instruction. One group of children was trained to sort words by meaning. A second group was trained to sort words according to their initial and final sounds while a third group was given this sound-based training and also taught to identify individual letters of the alphabet. Children who were given training in phonological analysis alone learned to read more successfully than the group who had been trained to classify words by meaning. However, the third group, who had received the sound training and had also been taught about letter-sound relationships, made even greater progress

The findings of the Bradley and Bryant training study were initially taken as strong evidence that children who were good at making judgements about similarities in rhyme and initial sound – often described as *rime* and *onset* (Goswami and Bryant, 1990) – were at a considerable advantage when they came to the task of learning to read. This finding has now been confirmed in many subsequent studies including Lundberg, Frost and Petersen (1988), Hoien and Lundberg (1988) and Stuart and Coltheart (1988). However, these later studies have also served to develop a more complex view of the relationship between phonological awareness and learning to read English.

Phonological awareness has now been shown to comprise two distinct skills each of which has a rather different relationship to reading skill. The first of these is *implicit phonological awareness* which is the ability to analyse words into their constituent sounds at the level of the syllable or sub-syllabic unit. The kind of tasks used by Bradley and Bryant in their training study – making judgements about the similarity of initial sounds and rhyme – involve implicit phonological awareness. As Bradley and Bryant (1983) and Lundberg *et al.* (1980) demonstrated, children who are good at making judgements about similarities of rhyme and initial sound before they go to school, tend to learn to read more quickly than children who are less good at these skills. However, implicit phonological awareness is only one of the skills required for learning to read. *Explicit phonological awareness* is also important

Explicit phonological awareness is the ability to detect and manipulate phonemes within words and, for this reason, it is often referred to as *phonemic awareness*. It is measured by performance in such tasks as phoneme counting (in which a child counts the number of phonemes in a word) and vowel substitution (where the child substitutes one vowel in a word with another). Phonemic awareness is important for learning to read because, once children can detect the individual phonemes in a word, it becomes possible for them to learn about grapheme–phoneme correspondences. Several studies (for example, Lundberg *et al.*, 1980; Stuart and Coltheart, 1988; Wimmer, Landerl, Linortner and Hummer, 1991) have shown that phonemic awareness develops as children learn to read. This makes it very different from implicit phonological awareness which develops before children start school and does not require any knowledge of reading or, indeed, any exposure to print. Success in phonemic awareness tasks predicts later success in reading and spelling (Hoien and Lundberg, 1988; Stuart and Coltheart, 1988; Wimmer, Landerl and Schneider, 1994).

Letter knowledge

Although phonemic awareness appears to develop in the process of learning to read, and as a result of exposure to print, some recent work suggests that letter knowledge may be an important precursor to this skill. One of the strongest advocates of the importance of letter-sound knowledge for reading success is Ehri (1987) who has argued that it directly paves the way for the development of an alphabetic strategy in which individual graphemes are recognized and their corresponding phonemes sounded out. She claims that pre-readers use visual or contextual cues to recognize a small number of environmental words, but that, as soon as children move on to reading, they rapidly shift to letter-sound cues. Although other authors have disagreed with Ehri's view of the speed with which children move on to an alphabetic strategy, there is good evidence that knowledge of letter names and sounds does underpin phonemic awareness.

Studies by Stuart and Coltheart (1988) and Johnston, Anderson and Holligan (1996) have found that children's knowledge of letters is a significant predictor of reading success for English; and similar results have been found for German by Wimmer *et al.*, (1991) and for Greek by Harris and Giannouli (in preparation). Harris and Giannouli also found that there was a strong association between letter knowledge and phonemic awareness (as measured by vowel substitution and phoneme counting) suggesting that these are, indeed, related skills. It is also relevant to note that, in the Bradley and Bryant training study described earlier, the children who learned to read most successfully were the ones who had been taught both implicit phonological awareness and letter-sound names. All these findings serve to illustrate the importance of letter knowledge for learning to read.

It is easy to see why learning the canonical sound associated with each letter could pave the way for both phonemic awareness and the development of alphabetic reading. The child who has a high level of implicit phonological awareness can divide a monosyllabic word into its onset (initial sound) and rime as in CH/AIR or SH/IP. However, in order to carry out a phonemic analysis, the child has to know that there are smaller units contained within the rime and onset which are based on letter sounds. Training in letter names and sounds can provide the child with an essential part of the knowledge required for this level of analysis.

Harris and Giannouli found that Greek children showed an improvement both in letter knowledge and phonemic awareness from the end of nursery school to first grade entry at the beginning of the new school year. They attributed this dramatic improvement to the fact that Greek parents teach their children the names of letters in order to prepare them for entry into the first grade of school, which is the point at which they are first given formal reading instruction. The success of this home teaching was evidenced by the finding that children entering the first grade knew almost all the letters of the Greek alphabet whereas children at the end of the nursery year, only four months earlier, knew very few.

Beginning to read in braille

Having established that both implicit phonological awareness and the ability to identify letters are essential components of success in the early stages of reading for sighted children, we can now consider the early stages in the development of braille reading. We will assume that both phonemic awareness and letter knowledge are equally as important for learning to read braille as they are for the initial mastery of print. However, there are reasons to assume that letter knowledge will take longer for blind children to develop and, if this is so, there will also be differences in the development of phonemic awareness.

One important difference between young blind and sighted children, as they first come to the task of learning to read, lies in the wealth of reading-related knowledge that sighted children bring with them. This is in marked contrast to the relatively impoverished pre-reading knowledge shown by most blind children at the time that they are first introduced to braille. Sighted children's knowledge comes from their experience of the written language, gained through exposure to books as well as to environmental print (for example, street names, road signs, labels on food and drink, and their own name) in the pre-school years. On school entry, many sighted children are not only able to recognize some words but they have also learned the names and/or sounds of some letters of the alphabet from teaching at home or nursery school. Pre-school blind children, on the other hand, receive little or no exposure to environmental print; their exposure to written language, in the form of braille, is often non-existent until they begin school at five years of age. Thus they come to school with no sight vocabulary, with little or no knowledge of how letters map onto sounds or even of what letters are: they must be taught each letter of the alphabet one by one. Blind children thus approach the task of learning to read with a much weaker knowledge base than their sighted peers.

Typically it takes blind children over a year to learn the braille alphabet in its entirety (Pring, 1994; Barlow-Brown, 1996). This is significant in two respects. First, and most obviously, it leads to a significant delay in reading development. Second, because each letter of the alphabet is taught individually in a pre-set order, this severely limits the reading material available to the child.

In the Royal National Institute for the Blind (RNIB) braille reading scheme, the first five letters introduced to children are B, A, G, L and I and all words that they are taught are initially made up only of these letters. In the UK, at the outset of learning to read, blind children are more or less restricted to the RNIB reading scheme books so they learn mainly these letters and a small number of words that can be formed from them (such as I, BAG, BALL, BILL and BIG). In stark contrast, sighted children continue to experience a wide range of books and written language both in and out of school and they typically have a greater selection of reading matter from which to gain information that will supplement their school experience. Furthermore, adults and older children can become informal reading tutors so, for sighted children, the entire reading experience can become an enjoyable activity that is shared with family and friends. Learning braille, by comparison, is much more likely to be a school-based activity which is shared with other people outside the school context only to a very limited extent. Thus the social and motivational aspects of beginning to read are likely to be very different for blind and sighted children. This is an issue of key significance but it has often been overlooked in the literature even though it is well established, for sighted children, that those who read more become better readers, rather than the other way around (Stanovich, 1986).

Learning braille letters

Having seen that there are important differences in the way that blind and sighted children first begin formal reading instruction, we now turn to a more detailed consideration of the way that blind children learn letters. In particular we can ask how blind children code individual letters in braille and whether this changes developmentally with time and experience.

In a recent longitudinal study, Barlow-Brown (1996) assessed the letter learning of six congenitally and totally blind children over their first year or two of learning braille. Every two weeks, letter knowledge was tested and recorded together with the letter recognition errors made by the children. These error data provided a detailed picture of how letter coding was taking place, and how this changed developmentally as the children began to learn more letters.

The study highlighted individual variations in the pattern of letter learning. Two of the children demonstrated a consistently slow rate of progression through the alphabet, whilst others demonstrated an exponential rate of learning, starting slowly and then learning new letters at an increasingly faster rate. This exponential pattern suggested the development of a new strategy for learning and remembering braille letters.

Support for this idea came from the pattern of error data which provided evidence of a change to shape-based coding at the time that the spurt in letter learning occurred. For the four children who showed a spurt in letter learning, errors initially bore no relation to the target letter. However, as the children suddenly learnt more letters, these no-relation errors were replaced by shape-related errors in which they confused letters of similar shape. This change in the type of errors made appeared to mark a shift in the coding strategy used to represent braille letters.

One interpretation of this new strategy was that it involved the children in discovering that there was a relationship among the form of all braille letters. This would be the case if they had become familiar with the form of the 2×3 braille matrix and had also discovered that all letters can be mapped onto it. Such a discovery would have important consequences for learning new letters because, as Millar (Chapter 4) notes, braille characters impose a great load on memory until they can be recoded.

Millar describes how recoding braille patterns as letters can significantly improve memory span. However, recoding at this level is only possible once a braille letter has been learned. Relating dot patterns to the braille matrix, that is, coding on the basis of overall shape, could be another way of reducing memory load and this would also be of use in learning new letters. A more effective strategy for learning new letters could then allow a sudden spurt in rate of letter acquisition, a pattern that was identified in four of the six children. If the use of shape-based coding does facilitate letter learning, then this suggests that encouraging such a strategy at an earlier stage could promote more rapid reading development. This possibility will be discussed at the end of the chapter.

The use of reading strategies by blind and sighted children

Given the differences previously noted in the early reading experiences of blind and sighted children, it might be expected that the early reading strategies of these two groups would be very different. However, if the early stages of learning to read are examined, some remarkable similarities can be found in the way that young blind and young sighted children learn to read, despite differences in their rates of letter learning.

Millar (this volume) suggests that beginning braille readers rely on letter-by-letter reading in which they pronounce the individual letters in a word. She claims that a similar pattern is shown by slow braille readers. The problem with letter-by-letter reading (which is also shown by some sighted adults with acquired dyslexia, see, for example, Warrington and Shallice, 1980; Kay and Patterson, 1985) is that successful word recognition requires phoneme blending, that is, joining the individual phonemes together to form a single word. This does not present a significant problem for languages such as Italian, Spanish or Greek which have a high level of orthographic regularity and a regular stress pattern. Children learning to read these languages can become fluent after only a very short period of reading instruction. However, for an irregular language such as English, phoneme blending is often problematic. This is because there is frequently not only ambiguity about which phoneme should be used to realise a particular grapheme but also ambiguity about how phonemes should be joined together to form a single word.

For English, familiarity with spelling patterns appears to be important for resolving ambiguities produced by attempts to sound out letters. Several authors (for example, Marsh, Friedman, Welch and Desberg, 1981; Frith, 1985; Seymour and Elder, 1986) have argued that sighted children first begin to read by building up a sight vocabulary of environmental words which are recognized on the basis of overall word shape (for a review see Beech, 1987). This stage appears to be particularly important when children are learning to read an irregular language like English in which there is an inconsistent relationship between letters and sounds. The next stage, according to Goswami and Bryant (1990), is that children go on to make use of their knowledge of rime and onset and to develop a strategy of reading by analogy.

Reading by analogy involves making comparisons among words that have similar spelling patterns. For example, a child who knows how to pronounce BEND and TENT may be able to read BENT using the analogy of the onset B in the first word and the rime ENT in the second. This use of larger units helps overcome some of the problems that are raised by the irregular pattern of grapheme–phoneme correspondences found in English.

For sighted children, then, both logographic reading and reading by analogy play an important part in the beginning stages of learning to read. Children also develop an alphabetic reading strategy in which graphemes are sounded out according to their equivalent phonemes. The evidence of letter-by-letter reading in blind children learning to read, and in poor braille readers, highlights the difficulty of using an alphabetic strategy alone for reading English. It also suggests, indirectly, that gaining information about spelling patterns is harder to achieve when children cannot use vision. One reason for this may be that visual access to words automatically gives information about overall word shape and orthographic patterns in a way that is difficult to mirror when access is through touch, particularly when there is an emphasis on phonics in braille teaching. This difficulty is exacerbated by the fact that, as noted earlier, blind children will probably have had no prior exposure to words and so will start to learn braille with no sight vocabulary. By contrast, most pre-school sighted children become very interested in words that appear in their environment and often begin formal reading instruction on school entry with a sight vocabulary of several words and many other words of which they have partial knowledge.

Early braille reading

The first study to look specifically at very early braille reading was a single case study of a young congenitally blind girl (Pring, 1994). This child began reading using an alphabetic strategy and did not exhibit logographic reading at all. From this, Pring argued that blind children learning braille might have more limited access to reading strategies than their sighted peers. However, this suggestion was not borne out by Barlow-Brown (1996) who found an interesting difference between the children in her study and the child studied by Pring. Evidence from Barlow-Brown's children suggested use of an initial strategy, based on logographic principles, that appeared before alphabetic decoding. This early strategy, termed an *audiogenic strategy*, appeared to be based on children's ability to remember words as rote spellings even though they were unable to decode these words phonemically. Having felt a word and then retrieved its spelling, the children could then use a salient letter, or the whole letter sequence, to access one of the limited number of words in their lexicons.

Barlow-Brown's study suggested that blind children, who are just beginning to learn to read, may develop two possible reading strategies. First is the use of learnt rote spellings, which form internal audiogens. This strategy bears a close resemblance to Frith's (1985) logographic phase of reading development. The blind child does not need to identify each letter within a word in order to activate a word's audiogen. Simply identifying a key letter is often enough to trigger the rote spelling which may then be used to identify the word. Errors will be made when the wrong audiogen is triggered; this may occur when one or more letters are shared between audiogens. The audiogenic strategy is common amongst early braille readers and it may be a by-product of teaching methods since blind children usually carry out repetitive spelling of words in their early reading vocabularies. The strategy becomes redundant quite quickly as the size of the reading vocabulary increases.

The second strategy is alphabetic and involves the use of phonemic information in order to read words using grapheme-to-phoneme rules. This strategy can be used instead of, in parallel to, or as a progression from, the audiogenic strategy. As noted earlier, children's phonemic awareness matures as they gain more reading and language experience, especially letter knowledge, and this paves the way for the use of grapheme-to-phoneme mapping. This strategy, which is the same as that reported by Pring, is equivalent to the one that characterizes Frith's alphabetic phase of reading development.

Once braille contractions are introduced, and possibly before alphabetic reading is fully developed, the child can use a third strategy. In part, reading contracted signs and words is closely related to the whole-word method of reading discussed in the sighted literature. Where a single sign stands for a word, the child needs only to learn and remember the direct correspondence between that and its pronunciation. Similarly, where one or two signs stand for an orthographic unit or sequence of commonly occurring letters, the child can use the information to identify the word without having a particularly deep or well-developed understanding of the written language and its correspondence with spoken language. This strategy is akin to reading by analogy. The difference is that, in the case of contracted braille, common orthographic strings (such as AND, ONE or ING) are formally marked by the use of a contraction and so should, if anything, be easier to spot than comparable strings used in print.

More research is needed to clarify the use and characteristics of this strategy of reading by analogy. Theoretically it could become available to blind children from the moment that the first contraction is introduced and so, in principle, it could be an early reading strategy. Consider, for example, the use of the single contracted sign for the word AND. This contraction is introduced fairly early on in reading instruction and it could enable the child to read such words as SAND, LAND or HAND. As with many words that are spelled using a contraction, children are typically unable to spell AND when it is first introduced, although they are able to use it in reading. The interrelationship of the various strategies that we have discussed is shown in a model of braille reading (see *Figure 5.1*).

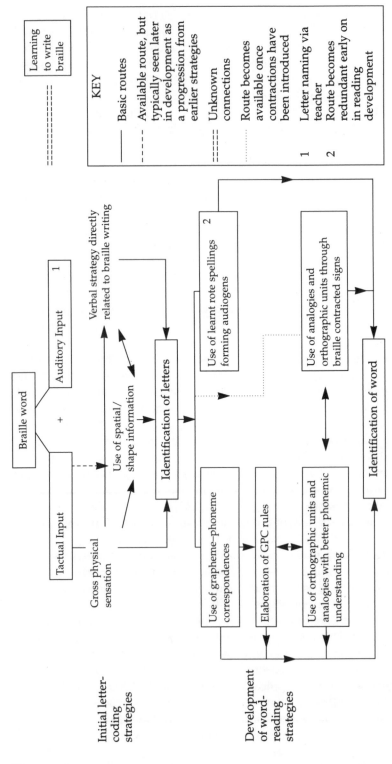

Figure 5.1 A proposed model of learning to read braille.

Teaching strategies for braille

Recent research on how sighted children learn to read has highlighted the important influence of teaching methods. Particular teaching methods can emphasize and encourage certain reading strategies rather than others. For example, a study in Scotland, carried out by Seymour and Elder (1986), found that children taught to read print by a whole word method used a logographic strategy when they first began to read. However, Connelly (1993) has shown that, if children are taught to sound out letters when they first begin to read, then they will pay much more attention to individual letters in words and will not use a purely logographic strategy.

When methods used for teaching braille are considered, it can be seen that the same general consideration applies. Indeed, given that braille learning is essentially a school-based activity, it might be assumed that the way in which braille is taught will have an even more marked impact on the way that it is learned.

One important aspect of braille teaching, described earlier, is the slow and structured manner in which the alphabet is introduced letter by letter and the very limited introduction of words that children spell aloud. As has already been pointed out, this may encourage rote learning of these words based on auditory memory of how they are spelt.

Writing braille

Another important aspect of braille teaching is the fact that learning to read braille is taught in parallel with learning to write it. As yet, the relationship between reading and writing braille is not understood. However, it is highly likely that the two processes are closely connected.

Braille letters are written by pressing a combination of six keys (one for each dot in the braille matrix) on a brailling machine. These keys are presented in a horizontal array although the matrix which they represent is vertical. This means that children have to learn to re-order the horizontal sequence (see *Figure 5.2*) in order to see the relationship between what they read and write. In order to write a letter, children are taught to associate each dot space with a number from one to six, as *Figure 5.2* illustrates. For example, the key on the extreme left (corresponding to the dot in the lower left corner of the braille matrix) is given the number 3 and the rightmost key (corresponding to the dot in the lower right position) is given the number 6.

This teaching strategy for writing braille has implications for the manner in which a child might learn to code letters for reading. Barlow-Brown (1996) describes children who used the key numbers as a way to remember the form of a particular letter. For example, one child remembered the letter U as the sequence 1, 3, 6 which corresponds to the numbers of the keys that have to be pressed to form that letter.

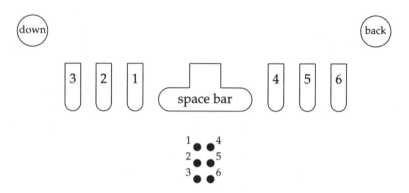

Figure 5.2. The Perkins brailler and the braille cell.

Unfortunately, the conclusions that can be drawn about the reading development of blind children are still somewhat limited by the small amount of research that has been carried out on the very early stages of learning to read braille. However, what can be seen already is that the picture is more complex than might at first be thought. There are important similarities in the early reading strategies that blind and sighted children develop and, in both cases, it is important to take account of individual differences among children. However, there are also important differences between learning to read print and learning to read braille. As already noted, these arise not only as a result of differences in the physical properties of braille and print, and the differing manner in which they are taught, but also as a result of important differences in the whole reading experience of blind and sighted children.

Becoming a skilled reader

Integration of information at an increasingly higher level becomes important as children move on to become skilled readers. Reading for meaning requires the integration of information across sentences to provide a coherent representation of a whole text. Again, the haptic modality poses its own special problems.

Studies of skilled sighted adult readers have highlighted the importance of eye movements for successful text integration (for a review, see Kennedy, 1987). For example, sighted readers can pick up a great deal of information in peripheral vision about the next section of text to be encountered. Thus, the skilled sighted reader will arrive at a section of text already knowing something about sentence boundaries and word length (which is a good guide to the presence of certain syntactic structures). Developmental studies show that sighted children gradually learn to read ahead in this way by bringing their forward eye movements under closer and closer control as they become more fluent readers.

Blind children who are learning to read braille will also have to develop a strategy for reading ahead if they are to become truly skilled readers. One possibility is that blind children can use one hand for reading braille and the second hand for scanning the text to the right. In her chapter in this volume, Millar describes two seven-year-old children who showed different levels of reading fluency. The more fluent reader read with her left hand and used her right hand for scanning ahead, pressing her thumb and forefinger together so that they formed 'a ridge which passed along the braille line'. According to Millar, this child was using the right hand merely as a place-keeper. However, it is possible that other readers may use the right hand to collect general information about word length and sentence boundaries in a way that is similar to sighted children.

Some pedagogical implications

The ultimate goal of learning to read is to extract meaning from text. However, in order to reach the goal of comprehension, children must first be able to decode individual words, and in order to reach the level of word reading, they must first be able to identify individual letters. Reading at this basic and initial level is sometimes overlooked. However, failure at this early stage has immense consequences for further development. Should a child struggle or fail at the outset of learning to read, then motivation and willingness to move forward will suffer as a consequence. For the blind child who faces more than enough obstacles on the path to successful reading development this has particular gravity.

If the task of letter coding could be made more efficient for blind children, and therefore the speed of letter learning increased, then there are important implications for the task of learning to read. Letter knowledge is an essential component of early reading success and so faster and more accurate identification of letters will pave the way for faster reading development.

As noted earlier, the most successful braille readers appear to be those who do not depend entirely on coding letters according to their gross physical properties but, instead, make use of the spatial pattern that each letter presents. Given this, there appears to be an unfortunate mismatch between what leads to successful learning and the method by which braille letters are taught.

One factor that contributes to successful learning of braille appears to be gaining an insight into the nature of the task. Barlow-Brown (1996; Barlow-Brown and Harris, 1996) described a series of studies which suggest that children can rapidly gain knowledge about the braille cell if they experience braille visually or through an enlarged tactile cell. This latter condition is appropriate for blind children and it involves the use of a pegboard to teach the children braille letters.

Barlow-Brown taught sighted pre-school, pre-reading children specific braille letters in one of four conditions. These conditions involved learning braille either visually or tactually, and in a standard or enlarged format. The two visual conditions produced more rapid letter learning than the two tactile conditions, suggesting that children find it more difficult to learn through touch than vision. However, there was an important difference between the two tactile conditions with children who were given large braille, using the pegboard, learning significantly more letters in a shorter space of time than the children who were presented with standard braille.

Following this training part of the study, all children were presented with the letters that they had been previously taught but this time in standard sized braille. Children who had learned braille visually were able to transfer the knowledge gained during the training sessions directly to a standard sized braille cell but the most complete transfer was shown by the children who had originally been taught large tactual braille using the pegboard. These children could transfer 100 per cent of the letters that they had learnt to the smaller sized braille.

Given this remarkable finding (Barlow-Brown, 1996), a study was then carried out to see whether the effects of using a large cell would be mirrored with a group of young blind children.

Research in the past has suggested that blind children may find it difficult to transfer information from a large cell to a small cell. Millar (1989) has argued that this is because there is a problem at the level of coding that does not make for easy transference of information across two sizes of braille. Barlow-Brown (1996) investigated transfer abilities directly in her study. She asked whether young blind children could be trained to learn specific braille letters in an enlarged form and then immediately transfer this knowledge to standard braille; and also whether they could recognize and produce letters in large braille format that were familiar to them in standard braille.

Barlow-Brown found that two young blind children, who were naïve to braille, were able to learn letters very quickly in an enlarged format and then to successfully transfer this knowledge to the standard cell. Older blind children, who knew some braille letters, could also learn new letters using the enlarged cell and, without any training, they could also recognize and produce familiar braille letters in this unfamiliar large format.

Assuming that these findings are confirmed with larger samples of children and with more letters, the two studies with sighted and blind children suggest that there is a great deal of benefit to be gained from the use of a large braille cell in the very early stages of learning to read.

It would seem that a large cell allows children to gain important information about the nature of braille that blind children normally realize only with a lot of time and braille experience. More specifically, our hypothesis is that a large cell leads to earlier use of shape as a coding strategy which, in turn, allows new braille letters to be learned more quickly. In addition, use of a braille pegboard would overcome the major problem of having to wait for blind children to develop fine tactile discrimination before they can be introduced to braille. Through an enlarged braille cell, children could be introduced to braille letters long before starting school. In this way they could be allowed to gain some of the essential pre-reading skills discussed at the beginning of this chapter.

Acknowledgement

The research on braille reading reported in this chapter was carried out while Fiona Barlow-Brown was in receipt of an ESRC studentship.

References

Barlow-Brown, F. (1996). Early developmental strategies used by blind children learning to read braille. Unpublished Ph.D. thesis: University of London.

Barlow-Brown, F. and Harris, M. (1996). Size does matter – new insights into how blind children learn braille. Department of Psychology, University of Southampton, Research Working Paper Series RWPS95/10.

Beech, J. (1987). Early reading development. In J. Beech and A. Colley (Eds), *Cognitive Approaches to Reading*. Chichester: Wiley.

Bradley, L. and Bryant, P. E. (1983). Categorising sounds and learning to read – a causal connection. *Nature, 301,* 419–521.

Connelly, V. (1993). The influence of instructional technique on the reading strategy of beginning readers. Poster presented at the VIth European Conference on Developmental Psychology, Bonn, Germany.

Ehri, L.C. (1987). Learning to read and spell words. *Journal of Reading Behavior, 19,* 5–31.

Frith, U. (1985). Beneath the surface of developmental dyslexia. In K. Patterson, M. Coltheart and J. Marshall (Eds), *Surface Dyslexia*. Hove: Lawrence Erlbaum Associates.

Goswami, U. and Bryant, P. (1990). *Phonological Skills and Learning to Read*. Hove: Lawrence Erlbaum Associates.

Harris, M. and Giannouli, V. (in preparation). Phonological awareness and learning to read and spell Greek. To appear in M. Harris and G. Hatano (Eds), *A Cross-linguistic Perspective on Learning to Read*. Cambridge: Cambridge University Press.

Hoien, T. and Lundberg, I. (1988). Stages of word recognition in early reading development. *Scandinavian Journal of Educational Research, 32*, 163–182.

Johnston, R. S., Anderson, M. and Holligan, C. (1996). Knowledge of the alphabet and explicit awareness of phonemes in pre-readers – the nature of the relationship. *Reading and Writing, 8*, 217–234.

Kay, J. and Patterson, K. E. (1985). Routes to meaning in surface dyslexia. In K. E. Patterson, M. Coltheart and J. C. Marshall (Eds), *Surface Dyslexia*. Hove: Lawrence Erlbaum Associates.

Kennedy, A. (1987). Eye movements, reading skills and the spatial code. In J. Beech and A Colley (Eds), *Cognitive Approaches to Reading*. Chichester: Wiley.

Lundberg, I., Olofsson, C. and Wall S. (1980). Reading and spelling skills in the first school years predicted from phonemic awareness skills in kindergarten. *Scandinavian Journal of Psychology, 21*, 159–173.

Lundberg, I., Frost, J. and Petersen, O. P. (1988). Effects of an extensive program for stimulating phonological awareness in preschool children. *Reading Research Quarterly, 23*, 263–284.

Marsh, G., Friedman, M. P., Welch, V. and Desberg, P. (1981). A cognitive–developmental approach to reading acquisition. In G. E. MacKinnon and T. G. Waller (Eds), *Reading Research: Advances in theory and practice. Volume 3*. New York: Academic Press.

Millar, S. (1989). Studies in braille. In R. F. V. Witte (Ed.), *Production of Hard Copy Materials for the Blind*. Marburg Lahn: Verlag der Deutschen Blindenstudien-Ansalt CV.

Pring, L. (1994). Touch and go – learning to read braille. *Reading Research Quarterly, 29*, 67–74.

Seymour, P. H. K. and Elder, L. (1986). Beginning reading without phonology. *Cognitive Neuropsychology, 30*, 1–36.

Stanovich, K. (1986). Matthew effects. *Reading Research Quarterly, 4*, 360–406.

Stuart, M. and Coltheart, M. (1988). Does reading develop in a sequence of stages? *Cognition, 30*, 139–181.

Warrington, E. K. and Shallice, T. (1980). Word-form dyslexia. *Brain, 103*, 99–112.

Wimmer, H., Landerl, K., Linortner, R. and Hummer, P. (1991). The relationship of phonemic awareness to reading acquisition: more a consequence than a precondition. *Cognition, 40*, 219–249.

Wimmer, H., Landerl, K. and Schneider, W. (1994). The role of rhyme awareness in learning to read a regular orthography. *British Journal of Developmental Psychology, 12*, 469–484.

Chapter Six

Social and emotional development of blind children: a longitudinal study

Gunilla Preisler

One of the major challenges for blind children is making friends, with whom they can share happiness, meaning, humour as well as secrets. If you ask a ten-year-old blind child whether he or she has a best friend, the most frequent answer will be that they don't. They might answer that they sometimes play with another child, but this often turns out to be a younger sibling. If you ask parents or teachers what they think the most severe or urgent problem is for a blind child, the answer is unanimous: social interaction and friendship with peers. These difficulties are also what we have observed when we have studied blind children in pre-schools and schools with sighted children. When we have asked professionals who provide educational guidance to parents or teachers in pre-schools and schools what they think the major task is for them as educators and as adults to achieve with respect to blind children's development, the most frequent answer has been: to enable them to manage on their own in order to make them autonomous.

Educational programs for blind children are primarily formulated for the training or teaching of motor skills, mobility, orientation, various perceptual skills, language learning, reading and writing in braille; that is, the focus is on the blind child's performance and skill, motor development and cognitive development. Attitudes towards performance and skill can be traced from the very first encounter between parents and the support system offered to them after their child has been diagnosed as blind or severely visually impaired. However, staff giving early parental guidance, or teachers in pre-schools or schools, seldom have a corresponding plan or curriculum for promoting the child's social and emotional development. The problems of social and emotional issues in blind children are well recognized by many of those who work with these children but theory is one thing, practice another.

The significance of early close relationships has long been assumed important for children's social and emotional development (Bowlby, 1982). Relationships are viewed as the context in which socialization takes place (Hartup, 1986), communication skills are acquired (Preisler, 1983), and the regulation of emotions develops (Stern, 1985). A secure relationship between child and significant caregiver is seen as not only the basis for the child's sense of self-efficacy and social skills, but also of key significance in the development of later close relationships (Bretherton and Waters, 1985). So, in thinking about the early socio-emotional experience of the child, it is also necessary to think about the caregiving relationship (Emde, 1989). Children develop as part of their everyday interactions within the family. The micro-culture of the parent–infant relationship allows the infant to take part in the macro-culture of the larger community (Fogel, 1993).

Social and emotional development in blind children

In this chapter some aspects of the social and emotional development of a group of blind children will be described, by following their development from infancy to pre-adolescence. Most of the data to be described emanate from a longitudinal, qualitative study of blind children, from infancy up to the age of six and then from a follow-up study when the children were 10 years old. The study started in 1982 and is still in progress (Preisler, 1990a; 1991; 1993; 1995; Preisler and Palmer, 1986; 1989; Elmgard and Thorén, 1988; Thorén, 1994). The children have been videoed from an early age, in different natural interactional settings in their own homes with their mothers and/or fathers. Interviews with parents have been carried out. When the children enter pre-school, video recordings were made in this new environment, and their teachers were interviewed (Preisler and Palmer, 1989; Preisler, 1993). At the age of 10, observations were made of the children in their schools, the children themselves talked about their lives, and interviews were carried out with the parents, teachers and others involved in the daily lives of the children.

In all, eight blind children have been studied from infancy to early adolescence. Three of them were born prematurely, two were born without eyes and three are blind due to congenital hereditary causes. The group consists of four boys and four girls. *Table 6.1* reports the children's medical diagnoses, age when diagnosed, and age at the first video recording. They live in rural as well as urban areas and come from middle class families. The group was representative of blind children born without known additional functional disabilities.

Table 6.1. Description of the blind infants participating in the study

Names	Diagnosis	Age when diagnosed in months	Age when entering the research project in months
Anna	Hereditary congenital retinopathy	3	3
Betty	Retinopathy of prematurity (ROP)	4 (1)	7 (4)
Caspar	Anophthalmia	At birth	5
Ed	Retinopathy of prematurity (ROP)	6 (3)	9 (6)
Fred	Hereditary congenital retinopathy	2	8
Ida	Anophthalmia	At birth	10
Jens	Congenital retinal degeneration	4	10
Karin	Retinopathy of prematurity (ROP)	5 (2)	24 (21)

Ages in parentheses have been corrected for prematurity
The infants' names have been altered to ensure confidentiality

The first two years

The infant enters the world with a biological preparedness for participating in social interaction. The parent is also prepared for social interaction in caregiving (Trad, 1990). There is no reason to believe that the situation is different in the case of a congenitally blind infant–sighted parent pair during the first weeks of life, before the parents even suspect that their child has a visual impairment. According to the parents themselves, the way they interact with and relate to their infant is probably very similar to the way most parents with newborn infants interact with and relate to their children. The blind newborn baby seems to exhibit all the characteristic expressions of a sighted newborn. At approximately two months the first suspicion may be raised about a visual impairment as the child does not give the same visual response as a sighted child. Diagnosis of blindness is seldom made before five months of age, except in those cases where there is gross malformation of the eyes.

The first five months

What are the characteristic features of a five month old infant? Stern (1985) maintains that, by the age of two to three months, infants begin to give quite a different impression of themselves. It is as if their actions, plans, affects, perceptions and cognitions can now all be

71

brought into play and focused for a while on an interpersonal situation. They seem to have an integrated sense of themselves as distinct and coherent bodies, with control over their own actions, ownership of their own affectivity, a sense of continuity, and a sense of other people as distinct and separate interactants. These experiences constitute a sense of a core self. The environment also starts to treat the infant as more social, more capable and more interested in social interaction. By the age of five months the baby is highly socially-oriented.

The affective changes that appear quite dramatically from two to three months of age give parents pleasure and incentives for continuing to be with their baby. Several investigators have described the interaction as having dance-like qualities (Brazelton, Koslowski and Main, 1974; Stern, 1985; Trevarthen, 1988).

Video, as well as direct observations of the blind children in the present study, at five months of age, showed that they were social and attentive to their mothers in the way that Stern has described as characteristic for this age period. They took part in proto-conversations, imitation was observed both from the parents and from the babies, and singing and playing or being with another person was preferred to manipulating toys or objects (Preisler, 1991).

But what can be observed with our eyes or focused on with the camera does not always reflect the inner emotional state of the mothers of the blind children. Even if they behave and act in a way that is characteristic of what mothers do with their infants at this age, their emotional situation is much more stressful compared to the situation of a mother with a baby without a functional disability like blindness. The way in which parents are told their baby is blind is for many parents a very traumatic experience which can affect their thoughts and feelings for a long period of time. (This has been described vividly by the Japanese Noble Prize winner, Oe, in his book *The Nightmare* (1994).) Nevertheless, emotions of insecurity, sorrow, worry, anger, guilt, and shame are mixed with feelings of relief (that it was only blindness), happiness that the child is alive and joy in interacting and playing with the child.

The parents' emotions are part of the parent–infant relationship. The part these emotions will play in the future depends at least in part on what personal and professional support the parents receive. So, even if the interaction might look harmonious and fluent, the parents' mixed emotions must be taken into account. Sroufe (1989) talks about how the caregiver crafts an organized system of co-ordinated behaviours around the infant at this age. But what if the parents lack this craft or strength? What support system is available for the parents after diagnosis? In Sweden, specially educated pre-school teachers will give parents advice on how to stimulate and facilitate the child's motor development, and also on how to stimulate their visual development in cases where there might be some residual vision. There is seldom a corresponding focus on social and emotional issues, such as ways to promote the relationship between mother and infant.

Six to fourteen months

At six to nine months of age, there is another major shift in the development of the sighted infant. The infant now starts to sit and crawl. With self-produced locomotion the infant's world changes again. Simple games begin with peek-a-boo and give and take with favourite toys. This relates to the comings and goings of caregivers as well as to the infants' beginning sense of understanding and coping with such experiences. In terms of an inner life, infants now develop a new organizing subjective perspective. They become more aware that there are other minds as well as their own (Stern, 1985). The sense of a subjective self and other rests upon different capacities for sharing a focus of attention, for attributing intentions and motives to others and apprehending them correctly. They can now share person–person–object awareness (Trevarthen, 1988). The sharing of affect is one of the main features of intersubjective relatedness. The mother now gradually starts to add a new dimension to her earlier imitation-like behaviour and expands her behaviours into a new category that Stern calls *affect attunement* (1985).

Observations of blind children at the age of six months show that mothers and infants start to share affect, and that the mothers, just like mothers with sighted children, start to use affect attunement behaviours. At this age, objects and toys are being introduced to the children. The blind children do not use gestures like pointing, either with their eyes or with their hands, or hand gestures like showing or giving. Such gestures enable caregivers to read the preferences and interests of a sighted child (Rowland, 1983; Urwin, 1978; 1983). The absence of co-ordination of eye-pointing with finger- and hand-pointing reduces the natural opportunities available for referring to external events. This apparent lack of attention towards the outside world by the blind child may discourage the caregivers from initiating activities involving external referents.

In terms of a sense of self, detailed analyses of video-recorded interactions indicate that blind infants, from the age of around nine months, show a growing awareness of a subjective and observable self, by demonstrating a realization that experiences can be shared with another person. They show their intentions and desires by vocalizations and body movements, but their expressions are not accompanied by mutual gaze or eye-pointing and therefore they are difficult for parents to interpret. Sighted children can read the emotions and intentions of their mothers from facial expressions, body postures and actions, and their own emotions and intentions can easily be read by the mothers in the same way. However, the reading of the other's emotions and intentions is not so easily accomplished in the sighted mother–blind infant pair

(Tröster and Brambring, 1992). Intersubjectivity means the meeting between two separate thinking, feeling individuals. Most sighted parents respond to their blind children's expressions in an appropriate and adequate way. But the parents must not only respond to their child, they must also show that they themselves have a will of their own, have their own intentions, feelings and expressions, which might be similar but can also be different from those of the child. Some parents seem to be more aware than others of the importance of being visible, or rather audible or readable to their children.

Fifteen to eighteen months

At around 15 to 18 months of age, infants begin to imagine or represent things in their minds in such a way that shows signs and symbols are now in use (Stern, 1985). When the infant is able to create shared meanings about the self and the world, a sense of a verbal self that operates in the domain of a verbal relatedness has been formed. Children now begin to utter their first words and to communicate verbally. According to Bates, Benigni, Bretherton, Camaioni and Volterra (1977), there are several good predictors of language development in sighted children, such as the pre-verbal gestures of pointing and showing; symbolic and combinatorial play; imitation and the use of tools. Observations of the blind infants showed that they did not use conventional gestures such as pointing with their eyes or hands. In some instances, pointing with the head or upper part of the body could be observed when the infants became attentive to sounds. But these means of communication were not always registered or even understood by their parents and therefore were not very effective means of communication (Preisler, 1991; 1995). Observations of the blind infants' play showed that they did not engage in pretend play during the infancy period. Some of the parents could be observed making efforts to involve their children in different sorts of symbolic play. However, the limited reactions from the infants discouraged the parents from continuing. Pretend play does not seem to appear until towards the end of the second year of a blind child's life (Fraiberg, 1977; Gustafsson and Preisler, 1991; Preisler, 1991).

Another pre-verbal predictor of language development in sighted children is imitation. The imitation possible for the blind child to engage in is primarily vocal imitation. In dialogue-like exchanges where parent and infant are vocalizing in turns, there can be imitative behaviours from both parent and blind infant. But compared to a sighted child, the possibility of engaging in imitative activities is very restricted for a blind infant. So is the use of tools. Compared to deaf infants, blind infants have fewer opportunities to take part in the external world (Preisler, 1995). This lack of experience of the external world might also explain the differences in the early use of verbal communication (Landau, 1983; Rowland, 1983). The age of onset of the first spoken words is later in blind infants as compared to deaf infants' first use of signs at around the age of six to eight months.

At the age of 18 months, blind infants can be observed to be involved in play with toys or objects with their mothers; that is, the external world starts to be included in the interaction. The children start to use single words when communicating with their caregivers. However, blind children are seldom reported to use two-word phrases before the age of two years (Warren, 1984; Bigelow, 1987; 1990; Mulford, 1988). In our studies, developmental differences between the blind children became more obvious from around 18 months of age, that is, between infancy and childhood (Preisler, 1995). This is the age when children start to walk and to talk, when they start to use symbols and when they begin leaving their parents physically as well as emotionally. But some of the blind children neither walked nor talked at this age and two of the girls did not start to use spoken language until the age of five years.

As the motor development of blind children is often delayed compared to that of sighted children during the first two years, support services tend to focus largely on gross motor functions at this age, such as sitting, raising to a standing position, creeping and walking. There is also a focus on the development of actions using the hands – grasping, reaching, giving and taking. This type of help is also requested by the parents, as they notice that their child's motor development is delayed. There is also emphasis on stimulating language, for example, labelling objects. Toys and objects are often introduced to facilitate both motor and language development. However, the focus is primarily on the needs of the blind child, seldom on the needs of the parents or the needs of the parents and their blind child together. The importance of conversations of feelings, of shared humour, and of connectedness are seldom stressed. These are described by Dunn (1993) as important dimensions in close relations and are probably part of a more general positive parent–child relationship.

The age between two and four

From the age of two and, in some cases, even earlier, sighted children start to talk about feelings, both their own and those of other people. They inquire and debate why people behave the way they do (Brown and Dunn, 1991); they begin to engage in conversations about themselves and other persons. Their world is widened as they walk, run and climb. They are already enrolled in different activities with peers in different pre-school activities. They engage in a variety of kinds of fantasy play.

Between two and three years

Many blind children aged two are still spending a lot of time exploring their physical environment. They explore different objects in their homes, especially in the kitchen and the bathroom. They use hands, faces and bodies in their exploration. They make comparisons, they investigate similarities and differences between sizes and weights (Gustafsson and Preisler, 1991). Those children who are actively exploring the world around them, not only the objects given to them, are doing this in close physical and emotional contact with their parents, most often their mothers. Just like a sighted child, they seem to be prepared to go out into the world, but need to come back regularly to a secure base. The blind children can now be observed to engage in pretend play with their parents: they can pretend that they are cooking food, or eating the prepared food.

From the age of two years, spoken language starts to be the main communicative means between parents and their blind child. Many parents express their relief as well as their joy when their blind child starts to talk. It seems as if a door is opening up to a new world of possibilities. The children can now be observed to initiate communication, to answer simple questions posed by their parents and some of the children in our study began to discuss their experiences and feelings: 'It feels very very nice' said one girl, aged two years two months, when she was exploring a smooth object. Some children became more autonomous at this age, and expressed their will, saying, for example, 'Don't want to'. Several children also began to use language to recall memories of past experiences.

The parents' physical and emotional presence for the blind children varied between different parent–child dyads. Some of the parents have been observed to be present, in every meaning of the word, by making comments on what the child is doing as well as disclosing their feelings about the actions; responding to the intentions of the child, and also telling the child about their own thoughts, feelings, intentions and motives. But some of the parents seldom talked about themselves or their feelings or thoughts; they did not share themselves with their blind child. Instead, they used a more directive communicative style which was less child-oriented (Thorén, 1994). This has also been reported in other studies of blind children at this age (see Kekelis and Anderson, 1984). From a blind child's perspective, it must be difficult to form a stable inner representation of another who is neither visible, nor showing her or himself in any other way.

Experience of other children

What experience of other children do blind children normally have at the age of two? Those with older siblings have experiences of other children from their own families. The presence of another child, who talks, who engages in pretend play, who quarrels, who shares their feelings and thoughts, gives the blind child an advantage in knowing what another child is, compared to a child without such experiences. The former will gradually understand that they are not the centre of the world and that they must share their parents' love and attention as well as share objects with somebody else. The older sibling can become their teacher, their audience and also a model for the blind child. The child can learn many of the rules of social interaction and social behaviour when it follows the older sibling and his or her peers. Those who are their parents' first child seldom have experiences of other children during their first two years and the social lives of the parents during these years seldom permit interaction with other families with children. It is also emotionally difficult to interact with friends who have sighted children, to see how easily their children's development seems to move from one milestone to another, milestones which are so difficult to achieve for a blind child.

When children are between one and two years of age, most mothers in Sweden return to work. All the mothers in our study work outside the home. At the beginning of the 1980s, the parents were recommended to send their two-year-old blind children to a pre-school with sighted children. When the children in our study started pre-schools at the age of two years, they met teachers with long and extensive experience of teaching young children. However, with a few exceptions, the teachers had neither prior experience of work with blind children nor with children with other functional disabilities. The teachers had been informed in advance by their employers (the county) that a blind child was going to be placed in their pre-school and they had also been informed about the child's needs by the child's parents and by an educational counsellor. They were offered a 3-day course at one of the two National Resource Centres for the Blind, and they were promised that a specially educated teacher would visit them regularly (Preisler, 1993). The physical environment in the pre-school was planned for sighted children and no special arrangements for a blind child were made initially. The sighted children at the pre-schools had no prior experience of blind children.

Several of the blind children who started in pre-schools at the age of two showed a marked regression in their development, physically, mentally, socially and emotionally. As a result, the recommendation in the 1990s has been to find alternative day-care for the children up to the age of three. At this age, many of the blind children can take part in simple conversations and they do not explore the environment as intensively as when they are aged between two and three. This exploration with hands, mouth, tongue and body can look very odd at times, and the teachers can be very confused as well as worried about these behaviours. They see them as stereotypies or at least as very odd behaviours that have to be stopped. By the age of three, many of the blind children seem to have a fairly stable representation of common objects. They start to use toys in a functional way or to use them in symbolic play.

For all the children in our study, the possibility of taking part in play or in other activities with sighted children depended to a great extent on whether it was structured, semi-structured or free play (Preisler, 1993). Structured activities, like listening to a fairytale, playing a game or meal-times were settings that the blind children seemed to enjoy most and where they could take part in a meaningful way. The teachers often took an active part in these activities, explaining the rules and elaborating their meaning. The children knew that each participant had to take their turn and should not talk at the same time as a peer. In most cases, the children were seated at the same place during these activities and were not moving around. For the blind child it was easier to follow the conversation, and, in some instances, to take part. In contrast, at the age of three, there were very few moments of spontaneous interaction between the blind child and the sighted children.

Between three and four years

According to Stern (1985), children in the age period between three and four start to be able to tell the story of their lives. They are entering the world of narratives and begin to develop a sense of a narrative self. The ability to tell their own story is linked to the development of object constancy and the earlier sense of self. It is a question of shaping self-biographies, of personal histories. The child now starts to look upon her or himself as an independent, autonomous and active individual, who has to fight for his or her position. The child becomes more aware of a time perspective. Observations of the blind children in their home environment showed how the children continued to explore the physical environment, experimenting and comparing forms and sizes, weights and sounds. They investigated concepts of 'inside' and 'outside', 'over' and 'under' and many others. Several of the children could now take part in fantasy play with the help of language. Some of them started to use the pronouns for 'I' and 'You' correctly. However, the children were not observed attempting to formulate their self-biography at this age. This started a year later.

For a blind child to develop positively, emotionally as well as socially, it is important that the parents make use of many of the same child-rearing principles they would use with a sighted child, to make the blind child aware of what is allowed and what is not allowed, and the consequences of their actions. Moral development is as important for the blind child as for the sighted. In relationships with peers, it is important that common moral principles are shared. If not, there is a risk that the blind child, in groups with sighted children, will be regarded as odd or different, or just nobody; a child to be ignored and therefore never part of social interaction with peers.

Fantasy play is an important part of both socio-emotional develop-ment and cognitive development. Adults can support the child's fantasy world, but must also be able to guide the child gently back to reality or even restricting fantasies which might carry the child too far away from reality and thereby become dangerous and anxiety-provok-ing for the child.

When the blind children were learning new words, sentences and expressions and their meanings and functions, some parents helped the children on their way, by translating, describing, and making the words and their meanings comprehensible, while others were not able to give the same support to their children. The blind children often played with words during this age-period; for example, putting an s-sound before every word; by making rhymes or in other ways experi-menting with words and expressions (Thorén, 1994). Once again it is important to guide the child gently forwards towards shared meaning and understanding. Otherwise there are obvious risks of confusion for the child.

The age period from two to four is a time when children want to make things by themselves, to dress and to undress, to do things in their own way at their own pace. Many of these activities are difficult to manage without sight, and this can make the child both frustrated and angry. They may also test the patience of parents. How much frustration can the parents manage? Conflicts observed were often of the same character as in sighted child–parent pairs. Many new ques-tions arise for parents in each new developmental period. What is nor-mal and what is not normal? What must the blind child be permitted to do because of the functional disability, what cannot be considered appropriate? Over- as well as underprotection are important issues to be defined and discussed in the upbringing of a blind child. Many parents need help and support to manage this difficult task, as they have no reference point when it comes to raising a blind child. But how often are normal child-rearing practices discussed with the parents of blind children? To my knowledge, far too seldom.

The age between four and six

At the age of four, the first traces of a narrative self emerged in some of the blind children. They could discuss past, present and future events in conversations with their parents and other adults. The discussions were not only recapitulations of what had happened or what was going to happen, but also what would have happened to them if the conditions had been altered. Several of the children started to show interest in the visitors – that is, in the researchers. They started to ask about us, which had happened rarely before. They wanted to show us what they were doing and they wanted to be seen. 'Can you see me now?' and 'Are you filming me now?' were sentences heard at this age.

Some of the parents supported the narrative child, supported the story to be told, while others did not support the telling of a life story, but rather supported the naming or labelling of objects, or different perceptual and motor skills. Observations from the pre-schools showed that from the age of around four, several of the blind children became aware of their own part in the group of children and also that what they said or did had an impact on the other members of the group. Several of the children found that if they uttered funny words or if they repeated funny actions, the other children started to laugh. Some of them became the clown in their group (Preisler, 1993). The blind children began to show an interest in taking part in semi-structured activities, like construction building. The frame of reference was set while the content of the interaction depended on the spontaneous actions of the children. In these interactions the blind child often listened to the sighted children's discussions and smiled when a child said something that they recognized or enjoyed. If there was any interaction between the blind child and the sighted children, it was often based on word-games or alliterations. There were seldom verbal exchanges of ideas or meanings between the blind child and the sighted children.

Problems in free-play

When the sighted children started to engage in free-play, all the blind children in the study had severe problems taking part and this continued throughout the pre-school period, which in Sweden lasts until children are seven. One problem in the free-play situation was to find toys that were interesting for the blind child to play with. Most of the toys at the nurseries were visually attractive and few of them were designed to stimulate senses other than vision in terms of function or material. During free-play the sighted children often moved around the room, talking and chatting to each other, and communicating by nonverbal means. They imitated one another's actions, and they communicated by facial expressions, body movements and, to a lesser extent, by verbal means. For the blind child it was difficult, or even impossible, to follow what was going on. Instead, they tended to withdraw to a safe place where they could interact with adults or where they were alone. From direct observations made in the pre-school settings, and from over 80 video recordings taken, we never observed the blind children spontaneously taking part in the sighted children's symbolic play or role play. With a few exceptions, the children were only observed to engage in symbolic play with adults. The content of this symbolic play was primarily based on auditory and haptic experiences, like pretending to wash clothes in a washing machine or washing in the dishwasher.

The most common way of trying to support the blind child's play with the sighted children has been to ask the sighted children to allow the blind child to take part in an on-going activity. In one case, however, a blind child's teacher reversed the situation and started activities with the blind child which were so attractive that the sighted children became curious and engaged, and finally asked if they could join in. Nevertheless, the most common situation was that the blind children spent most of their time at pre-school either alone or with adults. The time spent in interaction with other children could be counted in minutes per day. Again, the support given to the teachers mainly focused on the child's performance and skill, or rather *lack* of performance and skill. Much less support was given to relationships with peers.

Observations of the blind children between the ages of five and six clearly showed how many of the children now started to look like young schoolchildren. They could concentrate for extended periods of time on different tasks. They had started to read braille, they were interested in knowing which day it was, which month and which year. They could engage in conversations about the past as well as the future, for example what they wanted to do when they grew up. Many of them were in the process of formulating their life histories. But with growing self-awareness and with experience of attending pre-school activities with sighted children for several years, there was also a growing awareness of being blind or at least of being different.

The children at ten years

The blind children started school when they were seven years old, in some cases a year later. When they were 10 years old, further observations were made. This study is still in progress as not all of them have reached this age. Of eight blind children, diagnosed as *normal* blind children during their first 18 months, three of them have been diagnosed subsequently as autistic or showing autistic-like behaviours. Among the other five, there is considerable variation in emotional, social and cognitive development. The reasons for the developmental delays in some children and not in others are, of course, dependent on many different factors including personal and social factors in the families in which they grew up, as well as the child's constitutional factors.

Five of the children, two girls and three boys, are attending normal schools, two girls are integrated in classes with sighted children with learning difficulties, and one boy is in a special class for visually impaired children. The five children who are integrated in the normal school system do not take part in all the activities of the sighted children, and have many lessons alone with special teachers. It is still too early to say much about their progress in school, but some of them are making fairly good progress in reading and writing although less so in mathematics. They all make use of computers both at home and at school and now bring a small diskette back and forth between their homes and school, instead of the heavy books written in braille. Observations of the children in their classes, and interviews with parents as well as with their teachers, show clearly that, even if the children can take part in education in a normal school setting, they have difficulties taking part in social interaction with sighted children. The children also describe themselves as lonely children.

Discussion

This picture of the blind child's social and emotional development from infancy to pre-adolescence is rather bleak and pessimistic. What is the prospect for the future? In many respects it is difficult to grow up as blind in a sighted society. The blind child has to do so much more with so much less than a sighted child of the same age. There is also great stress put on parents and teachers to give the blind child a normal childhood as well as experiences which are adapted to the blind child's specific and unique situation. However, these intensive studies of individual children over a long period of time, with micro-analysis of data about child–parent, as well as teacher–child, and child–child interactions, combined with interviews and informal talks with parents, teachers and the blind children themselves, have clearly demonstrated the potential capacities of the children. From the videos it can be seen that the blind children repeatedly show the adults what they want and what they need. This is what developmental psychology has shown in studies of early normal infant development and this is valid for these blind children as well. They show their intentions and desires with body movements, with gestures, with facial expressions and with vocalizations when they are young. They develop these into actions, play and verbal utterances as they grow older. We have seen the same phenomena in studies of deaf children with parents and teachers, in multiply handicapped severely visually impaired children, and in deaf–blind children (Preisler, 1983; 1990b; 1994, 1996).

All of these children have something to tell. But we are not very good at noticing their questions and their propositions. Why do we not see and understand what they want to tell us? My belief is that it is because adults do not expect the children to know and understand as much as they do. Many adults still regard children as born with a mind like a *tabula rasa* and that it is the adult who is the giver and the child who is the receiver of information, particularly so if the child has a functional disability. The way the child organizes, interprets and creates experiences and the way the child then forges new relations are the products of their relationship history (Sroufe, 1989). Sroufe maintains that the child who can form a model, an inner representation, of a caregiver as available, caring, responding and understanding, will emerge with a complementary model of self as potent and capable. On the other hand, if the child has a history of insensitive care and rejection, or if the parents are emotionally unavailable, the child will suffer socially and emotionally and will form a model of self as isolated and unable to achieve emotional closeness.

When we discuss the blind child's socio-emotional development, we must look upon the child as part of a system of relationships, within the family, within the extended family, within society. If adequate psychological support is given to strengthen the relationship between parents and child and later between teachers and child, this will have an impact on the child's later functioning. The literature showing the importance of early relations, and of peer relations for subsequent individual development is quite compelling. If too much effort is concentrated on performance and skill, there is a risk that the child will be looked upon as an object, not a subject; that the child will be looked upon as some*thing* to form and create, not some*body* with his or her own intentions, feelings and motives. The functional disability will be in focus, not the child. This way of treating the blind child will later affect the sighted children in day-care centres and schools when they meet this child. Who wants to play with somebody who is nobody? If performance is stressed, the focus will be on evaluating accomplishments. But the young child does not want to be evaluated. The child wants to be seen and noticed. The child wants to share affect and joy. The child wants to form relationships. Therefore, for the future, the focus needs to shift from the individual performance of the blind child to the forming of relations between the child and the social environment.

Acknowledgement

The research reported in this chapter was supported by grants from the Swedish Council for Social Research.

References

Bates, E., Benigni, L., Bretherton, I., Camaioni, L. and Volterra, V. (1977). From gesture to the first word: On cognitive and social prerequisites. In M. Lewis and L. Rosenblum (Eds), *Interaction, Conversation and the Development of Language*. New York: Wiley.

Bigelow, A. (1987). Early words in blind children. *Journal of Child Language, 14*, 47–56.

Bigelow, A. (1990). Language in young blind children: Its relationship to their early awareness of their world. In S. A. Aitken, M. Buultjens, and S.G. Spungin (Eds), *Realities and Opportunities*. New York: American Foundation for the Blind.

Bowlby, J. (1982). *Attachment, 2nd ed.* London: Hogarth.

Brazelton, T.B., Koslowski, B. and Main, M. (1974). The origins of reciprocity: The early mother–infant interaction. In M. Lewis and L.A. Rosenblum (Eds), *The Effects of the Infant on its Caregiver*. New York: Wiley.

Bretherton, I. and Waters, E. (1985). Growing points in attachment theory and research. *Monographs of the Society for Research in Child Development, 50* (1–2, Serial No. 209).

Brown, J. and Dunn, J. (1991). 'You can cry, mom': The social and developmental implications of talk about internal states. *The British Journal of Developmental Psychology, 9*, 237–256.

Dunn, J. (1993). *Young Children's Close Relationships*. London: Sage.

Elmgard, M. and Thorén, A. (1988). *Språkliga strategier hos föräldrar till blinda barn* (Language strategies used by parents of blind children). Uppsala: Uppsala University, Institute for Applied Psychology.

Emde, R. (1989). The infant's relationship experience: developmental and affective aspects. In A.J. Sameroff and R.N. Emde (Eds), *Relationship Disturbances in Early Childhood*. New York: Basic Books.

Fogel, A. (1993). *Developing Through Relationships. Origins of communication, self and culture*. New York: Harvester Wheatsheaf.

Fraiberg, S. (1977). *Insights from the Blind*. New York: Basic Books.

Gustafsson, S. and Preisler, G. (1991). *Utvecklingen av lek hos blinda barn under förskoleåldern.* (The development of play in blind children during the preschool ages) (Report No. 59). Stockholm: Stockholm University, Department of Psychology.

Hartup, W.W. (1986). On relationships and development. In W.W. Hartup and Z. Rubin, (Eds), *Relationships and Development*. Hillsdale, NJ: Lawrence Erlbaum.

Kekelis, L. and Anderson, E. (1984). Family communication styles and language development. *Journal of Visual Impairment and Blindness, 78*, 54–65.

Landau, B. (1983). Blind children's language is not 'meaningless'. In A. E. Mills (Ed.), *Language Acquisition in the Blind Child*. London: Croom Helm.

Mulford, R. (1988). First words in the blind child. In M.D. Smith and J.L. Locke (Eds), *The Emergent Lexicon: The child's development of a linguistic vocabulary*. New York: Academic Press.

Oe, K (1994). *Mardrömmen* (The Nightmare). Stockholm: Norstedts.

Preisler, G. (1983). *Deaf Children in Communication*. Doctoral dissertation. Stockholm University, Department of Psychology.

Preisler, G. (1990a). The development of communication in blind infants. In S. A. Aitken, M. Buultjens and S.G. Spungin (Eds), *Realities and Opportunities*. New York: American Foundation for the Blind.

Preisler, G. (1990b). Development of communication in deaf infants. *Augmentative and Alternative Communication, 6,* 122–123

Preisler, G. (1991). Early patterns of interaction between blind infants and their sighted mothers. *Child: Care, health and development, 17,* 65–90.

Preisler, G. (1993). A descriptive study of blind children in nurseries with sighted children. *Child: Care, health and development, 19,* 652–672.

Preisler, G. (1994). Communication in sign – a challenge for the development of children with functional disabilities. In I.H. Pfusterschmidt-Hardtenstein (Red.) *Was is der Mensch?* Wien: Ibera.

Preisler, G. (1995). The development of communication in blind and in deaf infants – similarities and differences. *Child: Care, health and development, 21,* 79–110.

Preisler, G. (1996). Patterns of interaction between deaf–blind children and their parents. In A.M. Vonen, K. Arnesen, R.T. Enerstvedt and A.V. Nafstad (Eds), *Bilingualism and Literacy Concerning Deafness and Deaf–blindness.* Sküdalen Publication Series No 1. Oslo: The Research and Development Unit, Sküdalen Resource Centre.

Preisler, G. and Palmer, C. (1986). The function of vocalization in early parent–blind child interaction. In B. Lindblom and R. Zetterstrîm (Eds) *Precursors of Early Speech.* Wennergren International Symposium Series, *44,* 269–277.

Preisler, G. and Palmer, C. (1989). The blind child goes to nursery school with sighted children. *Child: Care, health and development, 15,* 484–492.

Rowland, C. (1983). Patterns of interaction between three blind infants and their mothers. In A.E. Mills (Ed), *Language Acquisition in the Blind Child.* London: Croom Helm.

Sroufe, A. (1989). Relationships and relationship disturbances. In A. Sameroff and R. Emde (Eds), *Relationship Disturbances in Early Childhood.* New York: Basic Books.

Stern, D. (1985). *The Interpersonal World of the Infant.* New York: Basic Books.

Thorén, A. (1994). *Språk och samspel mellan blinda barn och deras föräldrar.* (Language and interaction between blind children and their parents.) Licentiate thesis. Stockholm University: Department of Psychology.

Trad, P.(1990). *Infant Previewing.* New York: Springer.

Trevarthen, C. (1988). Infants trying to talk. In R. Sîderbergh (Ed.), *Children's Creative Communication.* Lund: Lund University Press.

Tröster, H. and Brambring, M. (1992). Early social-emotional development in blind infants. *Child: Care, health and development, 18,* 207–227.

Urwin, C. (1978). The development of communication between blind infants and their parents. In A. Lock (Ed.), *Action, Gesture and Symbol.* London: Academic Press.

Urwin, C. (1983). Dialogue and cognitive functioning in the early language development in blind children. In A.E. Mills (Ed.), *Language Acquisition in the Blind Child.* London: Croom Helm.

Warren, D. (1984). *Blindness and Early Childhood Development.* New York: American Foundation for the Blind.

Chapter Seven

Seeing and being seen

Alan Fogel

Most blind children go on to live in a sighted world and to be productive citizens in that world. They can learn language and they can become participants in most realms of a tolerant society. However, there will always be a difference between the psychological experience of the blind and the sighted, and it is a difference that will not, and, as will be argued in this chapter, should not, disappear. This chapter will expand on Preisler's main point (Chapter 6), that the reason many blind children develop psychosocial disorders lies somewhere in the mismatch between their unique experiential world and the educational system that presumes to understand what is best for them, by examining some examples related to the experiences of the visually impaired and the sighted and the role of sight in human relationships.

The psychology of the visually impaired

It is clear that the sensory systems, even when all are intact, are not equivalent. They are not simply passive routes into the brain, but have experiential features that are different from each other: flavour does not reduce to colour, colour can never be captured in a melody, and a loving touch can be compared to nothing else.

Descartes (as quoted in Gregory, 1966) described a blind person tapping with a stick while walking as follows, 'You will find that they feel things with such perfect exactness that one might almost say they see with their hands'. The important word in this sentence is 'almost', because if you think about how you see with your hands when you explore an object with your eyes closed or explore the world around you in the dark, the experience is different from visual experience. If sight is not used, similar conclusions may be reached about the form of the object, and it may be possible to navigate through space in roughly the same way as if using sight. While the result is 'almost' the same, the actual experience of sensing and acquiring the knowledge is not the same.

Vision is based on continuous experience. Depth is seen, whole objects are seen, multiple shapes are seen, one shape can be seen to include another shape. Vision has a continuous flow that includes colour and depth, closeness and distance, and a quality of immediacy that the other senses do not have.

With touch, the whole cannot be taken in at a glance, an entire field of objects cannot be felt. In any particular lived moment of experience, only a small part of a single object can be taken in, and the only objects which can be taken in completely and continuously, in a manner akin to visual immediacy, are objects that are small with respect to the size of the hand. To acquire information about space or other people or objects through touch requires a series of steps. Touch is a sequential sensory system, whereas vision is a simultaneous and continuous sensory system. Touch, more so than vision, is like the experience of communicating with language, which is a sequential series of communicative actions. Vision, more so than touch, is like the experience of communicating non-verbally, as in dance where sequential movements evolve out of the immediacy and continuity of co-movement.

The mind–body system for the visually impaired

In a dynamic psychological system, cognition and emotion are different in the company of different sensory systems. In *The Body in the Mind*, the philosopher Johnson (1987) suggests that our modes of cognition are fundamentally dependent upon the body modality through which the experience is acquired. Thus, there is not one, but many forms of cognition, each of which comes into being in relation to the specific palette of sensory experiences available.

In what way could the cognition of the blind person be different from the sighted person? The writer and author Swan has commented on the radically different phenomenological worlds of the blind and of the deaf. He writes, 'The blind woman's walk through the world is an intensely narrative activity, a continuous exercise in memory and prediction' (Swan, 1992). In her autobiography Helen Keller wrote, 'My fingers cannot of course give the impression of a large whole at a glance but I feel the parts and my mind puts them together' (Keller, 1908). When one thinks about narrative storytelling, it comes in bits, it comes in steps. It is only interpretatively, over time, that one finds the meaning of the narrative.

The sequential modalities, touch and audition, require an interpretative or narrative form of cognition. Vision is more analytical. Parts and wholes can be seen all at once and it goes easily with a cognition that is more conceptual, one that breaks things into constituent parts. These two modes of cognition, the narrative and the paradigmatic (formal, analytical), have been described as separate ways of knowing, one not more or less important than the other (Bruner, 1986).

Fraiberg (1977), suggested that blind babies, even at four or five months of age, were capable of narrative type cognition: interpretatively filling in the blanks between their sequential experiences. The sighted baby who reaches for and attains an object at four and a half months does not need a concept of an object to do this. The blind infant may indeed have a concept of the object, but it is not a visual concept of the object as having a separate identity, standing apart from other objects (Gibson, 1993). Rather, the object is identified as embedded within a flow of narrative-like sequential action in the context of an ongoing relationship with the object. If the whole child is considered, that is, the whole psychological system of perception, cognition, and emotion, we are likely to see very different kinds of normal development in the blind compared to the sighted. The result is a uniquely human individuality.

Normality is not defined by a particular sensory system, whether it is functional or not, or a particular type of cognition, or a particular form of emotional experience. Rather, to develop normally what is required is a dialectic between perception and cognition and emotion. It is in the crucible of the dialogue within one's self, and between one's self and the environment, that functional action is created. Action is the result of a complex system of constituents, constituents that change each other in the process of creating a whole; it is not the simple read-out of any single constituent. Action is neither sensory nor cognitive, motor nor neural. Rather, it is the combined effectances of the whole person in the context of their living narrative relationship with the world.

On seeing and being seen

Part of what leads me to this perspective on the normality and uniqueness of the blind child's development comes from my own personal experience: I am partially visually impaired. Without my glasses, I am unable to resolve images clearly beyond 20 centimetres from my face. Outside of that distance the world is a muddle of indistinct shapes. At greater distances, beyond three metres, depth perception is lost and even colours become greyed and muddied as they bleed into each other. Although I have never studied blind or visually impaired children, I have the recollections of my early life, before my vision was corrected at the age of nine years.

Before that age, during my first three years in school, I was diagnosed as a difficult child. My school, in a working class neighbourhood in steamy Miami in the early 1950s, was not very sophisticated: if you were marked as a problem, you were likely to stay that way as increasingly hostile reactions from teachers and peers confirmed and amplified the difficult behaviour, which then became the only recognized means of making at least some kind of human contact. In the third grade I moved to a different school in the same neighbourhood. My enlightened teacher suggested to my parents that I might have a visual impairment, and she recommended an eye test.

After a visit to the local optometrist, I was prescribed an enormous correction. In those days we had neither tempered glass nor high impact plastic, so that meant thick and heavy lenses mounted into chunky fleshy frames. I came to hate these glasses as a symbol of my deficit, and because they made me the target of name calling by the class bullies.

On the day the glasses were ready I convinced my parents to let me go alone to the optometrist, a bicycle ride of 20 minutes. I waited in the outer office lit by a large window. It overlooked the main street of the village of Miami Shores, lined with trees, small shops, a café, and the Shores Theatre where hundreds of us passed most of every Saturday watching cartoons, shorts, and feature films with a packed lunch and enough money for admission, popcorn and candy. I always sat close to the screen to enlarge the total effect, and, I suppose, so I could see at all.

The optometrist, a soft-spoken man in his forties, came into the waiting area holding a pair of glasses in one hand and reaching out to shake my hand with the other. His respect for me as a real person never waned over the many following years of eye examinations, increasing prescription strengths, broken and replaced glasses. 'Let's go outside. I have something I want to show you', he said. Once on the sidewalk he turned me to face the opposite side of the street while he stood behind, guiding me with a hand on my shoulder. In an anticipatory tone, he said, 'You won't believe what's going to happen. Close your eyes'. I waited in the sunny darkness as he brought the glasses over my head and slipped them over my ears and nose.

'Open your eyes and look across the street', he whispered. 'Look at the sign in the store window'. From the window facing the opposite sidewalk the letters jumped off their gold plate backings and vibrated red in empty space: SHORES CYCLES. 'Look up the street', was the next command. There was the movie marquee with the show times in fine clear print. On the street I could see people's facial expressions, a traffic signal with three distinct changing colours, bright textured clouds skimming over the trees. And then for the first time I saw a tree from a distance. I had snuggled up to trees in endless climbing, I had a tree fortress in a huge rubber tree in the back garden. I had studied the cellular structure of a leaf under a microscope. I knew trees up close, and here, now, was a whole tree seen from afar.

Because my near-sightedness trained my eyes for vision during my early years, I was able to organize the jumble of visual sensations into recognizable images. If I had been completely sightless, I would only have seen the jumble. Even though I did not have to learn to see, I was not ready emotionally for the world at a distance to become so suddenly real, so incredibly compelling. Without my usual deliberations, my gradual pace, my regulated steps, I become overwhelmed, withdrew, and wanted to retreat into the comfortable nearby world and to deny what I already sensed was a life-changing discovery.

The inner world of the blind is more withdrawn and receptive than that of the sighted. When asked to describe their experiences, both the blind and the sighted report similar kinds of emotions. The situations that precipitate the emotions are different, however. In the emotion of joy, for example, sighted people mention active experiences of self-initiated enjoyment while blind people mention situations in which they receive something gratifying. Sighted individuals mention interpersonal conflicts as a source of anger, but this is rarely mentioned by the blind who take a more accepting approach to interpersonal contacts. The blind, then, keep themselves at a psychological distance from emotional situations. When asked to recall emotional events, they refer to situations in the more distant past than the sighted (Galati and Cattaneo, 1995).

The sculptress, Ann Truitt (1982), in her diary, *Daybook*, reports an early visual impairment similar to my own. Her near-sightedness was discovered for the first time when she was in the fifth grade. She credits her early engagement in the near environment, detached from the distant, as accounting for at least part of what she calls her 'interiority'. I also share with Truitt a sense of psychological interiority, which in my case is manifested by a predilection for thinking and evaluating before acting. As Fraiberg (1977) suggested, the visually impaired may develop precocious forms of narrative intelligence. This narrativity of my psychological world, this sequentiality, made for deliberate rather than spontaneous action. From an early age, I had the appearance of timidity: a reluctance to engage in anything I could not understand before the fact of actually engaging in it.

This experience of reluctance during my first nine years created the basis of a reclusive self. I still prefer to prepare for events mentally before I engage in them: I read the instructions, I take the lessons, and I deliberate. As a child in interpersonal situations which I could not control or predict, I was painfully shy. I would hide under my bed or in my cupboard, or I would disappear into the bushes when a guest arrived. An advantage of shyness at an early age is that one develops a relative sense of independence from other people. The disadvantage is that one learns to live somewhat apart from the network of family and peer relationships and one loses the means for connecting with them in deep emotional ways.

I also remember feeling afraid of getting caught in the act of doing something inappropriate. Although I cannot be certain, I believe that this too was partially related to the visual impairment because I could not clearly see the facial expressions and gestures of other people. I remember that when talking with adults in particular, I would look down and away from the person: an attitude of submission. I think that this posture of staring off into distant space occurred because it was less confusing for me simply to hear the voice of another person and not look at the blurry face. This, however, put me at a disadvantage. First, I could not anticipate the actions of others because I was not looking at them, nor could I see them clearly even if I looked in their direction. Second, I learned to be submissive not only in posture but in spirit as well. And finally, I was indeed caught revealing something about myself that I did not know I was revealing. People could see things about me that I could not see about them, and in the resulting confusion I became even more guarded emotionally. I did not realize that there was a limit to what others could see inside of me. Childhood naïvety led me to conclude that being seen by another person was a violation of my integrity, a knife thrust deep into the psyche.

I had few friends in school where they did not understand me, and many friends in my neighbourhood where I was able to express myself in active play, in contact sports, in long talks sitting with friends on those endless warm evenings. Uncorrected myopia makes movement and touch essential. In the words of Truitt, 'I think that because I couldn't see, I was forced to develop my kinaesthetic senses towards a perhaps unusual acuity' (Truitt, 1982).

In school, I was unable to comprehend events in the front of the classroom out of my focal range and I acted out various forms of mis-behaviour in the near environment. I would pull the hair and poke the back of the person sitting in front of me. I would carve and colour my desk. I would chase girls in order to hug and hold them. I would sing and talk to myself while sitting in the classroom. I would have seemed an odd and perverse child in that tropical grade school almost half a century ago. Part of my misdeeds can be explained because my own talents went unrecognized in the context of a traditional classroom, talents that had been recognized in my family and in my network of neighbourhood pals.

Often, visually impaired children may seem aloof and defiant because they have come to trust themselves in special ways that other children do not know about or understand. Such children are not defi-cient, they are precocious. Precocity can lead to early self assurance in a medium in which the child has developed a special skill. In the best of conditions, these budding skills are recognized by parents and teachers and they become part of the child's identity. This recognition amplifies the initial precocity and allows the child to develop those abilities further. For children who are different, many of their misdeeds declare the need to be seen by others as a complete and worthwhile person, to be seen with a loving rather than a cutting gaze.

In her chapter (this volume), Preisler talks about 'being seen', a metaphor for a deep, loving human communication. Like vision in physical space, being seen embraces the depths of psychic space. One does not have to be sighted, however, to be seen or to see someone as a whole person. Preisler concludes that parents and teachers should look upon the blind child as 'somebody with his or her own intentions, feelings and motives . . . The child wants to be seen and noticed. The child wants to share affect and joy. The child wants to form relations'.

Earlier in this century, the philosopher Buber made a similar point regarding education. The genuine educator,

sees individuals as in a position to become a unique, single person, and thus the bearer of a special task of existence which can be fulfilled through him and through him alone. He sees every personal life as engaged in such a process of actualization (Buber, 1992).

Being seen, in this sense, is like being spoken to by someone who recognizes your status as a person. It is a recognition that people are different, and that changing another person into something they may not wish to become is no longer education, but propaganda for the teacher's own point of view.

Oliver Sachs (1993), the author-neurologist, has described the case of Virgil, who was blinded since early childhood by thick cataracts. Virgil had settled into a comfortable, if bland, life of blindness in which he knew his way around. This all changed when his fiancée convinced him to undergo an operation to remove the cataracts. She thought, at least from her sighted perspective, that this would open up a whole new world to Virgil. It was her world and she wanted to share it with him.

It is clear from research on the acquisition of sightedness in adults who have been blind since early childhood that knowledge of the world is learned (Gregory, 1966). One must have experiences of moving and acting in a sighted world in order to appreciate and interpret visual sensations. In hundreds of documented cases, when a childhood onset visual impairment is removed in adulthood, the individual is inundated with incomprehensible sensations. Not only that, the newly-sighted are often confused and frightened by what they see and they cannot connect it to their narrative world of touch and sound.

For Virgil, the result was the same. Several months after his surgery he reported feeling more disabled than when he was blind. One cannot replicate a lifetime of visual-motor experience within a few months or years. Virgil became depressed and he stopped learning how to see. He eventually returned to the patterns of behaviour that had sustained him when he had been physically blind: his auditory–tactile narrative way of knowing. He chose to act blind, and his family had to accept that there was no other way for him to be. As Sachs put it,

Now, at last, Virgil is allowed not to see, allowed to escape from the glaring confusing world of sight and space, and to return to his own true being, the touch world that had been his home for almost 50 years (Sachs, 1993).

Virgil is a parable for the inevitability of developmental history to constrain activity in the present. There are many cases in the annals of psychology attesting to the power of an individual's past and the traumas of their childhood to forge a lasting imprint on the adult psyche. The case of Virgil also illustrates the profound relation of the body to the psyche. Impairments in the peripheral organs of the body, after they enter into the stream of the individual's developmental history, become absorbed into and integrated with the psyche (Fogel, 1996). Once this mind-making process has run free for a few years, the psyche of the visually impaired person can never become like the psyche of the sighted person.

The contributions of sensory experiences to the psyche are made more salient in those who have suffered sensory impairment. In my own case of early childhood visual impairment, in spite of most of a lifetime of fully corrected vision, I have never escaped the feeling that touch and sound are more real, more sensual experiences than vision. I often have the feeling of *not believing my eyes*. When I look at a mountain landscape, I cannot psychologically connect with it until I have the opportunity to walk in those mountains and touch the earth. I feel the most *myself* during athletic activities, listening to music, and when I speak or write (tactile and auditory narrative-sequential media). In these activities I am being seen by myself.

A blind child, not knowing the socially acceptable ways of expressing this need for touch, sound, and movement, may, as Preisler (Chapter 6) points out, appear peculiar, and potentially confusing, to a sighted person. The activities and movements the children make, seemingly unschooled, unsocial activities, make it difficult to see the blind child's basic individuality. Preisler (Chapter 6) describes how young blind children's exploration of the environment 'with hands, mouth, tongue and body could look very odd at times'. For the sighted, it is difficult to connect with the person performing these acts.

The blind in a sighted culture

These examples suggest that sensory organizations are fundamentally embedded in social orders. For this reason, sensory processes can be thought of not as things that belong to individuals as biological properties, but as components of cultural systems, where culture is a system of interpretations and valuations of everyday experience.

To be blind is like being a member of a racial or ethnic minority: the blind are different from the mainstream in a way that they cannot change. They are not only physically different but culturally different too. Currently the culture of the blind is relatively impoverished because, in a sighted world, it is not allowed to develop. The culture of the deaf, enhanced by having its own language of signs, is relatively farther ahead in its self-definition and self-understanding than the culture of the blind (Swan, 1993).

If blindness is not an impairment, but rather an entrée into a different culture, then the sighted who attempt to communicate with a member of the blind culture may feel like foreigners in a strange land. It is difficult to appreciate the nuances and depths of a culture when your most immediate impression is frustration that things do not work the same as in your own. This must also be similar to what blind children feel in their everyday lives, as intruders in the sighted culture which struts its sense of superiority.

Cultures vary in their explicit recognition of the importance of touch, rather than vision, as a modality of interpersonal communication. There is a good deal more touching, for example, in the Latin cultures of Southern Europe and South America than there is in Northern European and North American cultures. In a recent study (Franco, Fogel, Messinger and Frazier, 1996), nine-month-old infants from Hispanic American families were compared with infants from Caucasian American families. A great deal more touching was observed between mothers and babies in Hispanic American families. In the Hispanic American families, there was virtually constant physical contact, usually with a lot of hugging, kissing, and touching.

The blind baby needs some sort of continuous interpersonal flow of experience that is comparable to vision, and that must be achieved primarily through audition and touch. Studies of blind infants living in northern cultures have shown that they lag behind sighted infants in most indices of infant development, even those involving touch and sound (Fraiberg, 1977; Hatwell, 1994; Masini and Antonietti, 1994). Although Franco et al. (1996) did not study visually impaired children, it seems likely that blind babies in Hispanic American cultures may develop tactile abilities more fully than blind babies from less contact-oriented cultures. Since this tactile experience is bound up with a continuous interpersonal relationship with the parent, one might expect it to spill over into all realms of development.

Mutual, interpersonal touching, as a continuous background for communication should, theoretically, serve the same role as continuous visual contact: the sense of engagement, an awareness of the loving presence of the other person, and a shield against loneliness and depression. Interestingly, there is support for this idea from

observations of a non-human species. These observations were reported in an article in the *Salt Lake Tribune*, in Salt Lake City, Utah, in
August 1995. Utah is part of the former Wild West of the United States
and there is still a great deal of wilderness there, wide open lands that
no longer exist elsewhere. The article described herds of wild horses
that roam in Utah, Colorado, Nevada, and Wyoming living primarily
on government protected land. A group of government field biologists
had been observing a particular herd of wild horses in Southern Utah
for many years because the horses used an unusually large number of
vocalizations with each other. The biologists captured a few of these
horses and discovered that some of the horses were blinded by
cataracts. The article reported an interview with field biologist Gus
Warr, a wild horse specialist for the Bureau of Land Management.

After observing the animals for thousands of hours, Warr realized the nearly
blind horses whinny and wait for responding calls from animals with good
sight. A horse with good eyesight picks out a trail that is easy for the blind to
follow. And when running, the blind horse will sometimes lean its head
against the hind quarters of the 'seeing-eye horse' (Law, 1995).

This is a powerful example of how the sensory systems in the body
become part of the social order. There is a changed communication
system between the animals that creates a new kind of social order that
was not there before, was not there without the blindness. In this herd,
the individuals are now touching more than they would have otherwise and they are now vocally calling more than they would have if all
of them were sighted. What might be the experience of the blind horses
and the sighted horses in their relationships to each other?

The way people feel, about their body, about their vision, about their
touch, about their actions, thoughts and feelings, is fundamentally
caught up with the way their partners relate to them and whether they
are seen as a whole person (Fogel, 1993). Research on socio-emotional
development shows that people accept and develop those parts of
themselves that are embedded in relationships of love, trust and
attachment. People deny and defend against those parts of their histories that have arisen in the negativity of coercion, those parts that have
not been seen by anyone.

It is important to think about the world of blind individuals, to relate
to them as whole people, to enter into their different culture; it is just like
going to another country and struggling to speak the language and trying not to use gestures that are offensive. It is crucial to figure out what
it is about that culture that will allow sighted people to relate to blind
people or to become participants in their culture. This cultural approach
to blindness is one of the contributions of Preisler's research which has
been based on a qualitative longitudinal investigation of children in
ongoing relationships. Qualitative research is a means of capturing

experiential meaning and the individuality of the behaviours that are observed. It allows behaviour to be put into a cultural and interpersonal relational context by means of a principled, hermeneutic interpretation.

The idea that the body and the sensory system are embedded in social processes also suggests that interpersonal relationships with sensory impaired people are different than relationships with people who do not have sensory impairments; relationships between blind and sighted individuals are different than between two blind individuals or two sighted individuals.

Epilogue

In the course of this chapter, I have told you something about my own childhood and its effect on my present psychological processes. I would like to end with some thoughts about the future.

I know that I am losing my vision. It is slow, and will take ten or more years, assuming I live that long. My ophthalmologist told me, during my most recent eye examination, that my lenses are becoming cloudy, the initial signs of cataracts. My mother, who lost the vision in one of her eyes due to a torn retina when she was a young adult, had a tense cataract surgery on her only good eye in her early seventies. My brother had cataract surgery in his late forties. Visual impairment, in one form or another, is in the family gene pool. Already, at age fifty, I observe my vision deteriorating. I cannot see clearly at a distance even while wearing my glasses. I had come to accept the inevitability of cataracts and the prospect of surgery.

However, now I realize that, like Virgil, I have a choice about whether I want to live my life with a visual impairment. If I were blind or nearly so, I could return to the world of my childhood; I could appreciate it better now and as a trained psychologist. I could give up the visual world, whose liberating simultaneity and spontaneity I have never fully trusted. Being blind, I might learn to see beyond the superficial, given so glibly by vision.

The power of seeing beyond the superficial is evoked by Derrida (1993) in *Memoirs of the Blind*. Derrida discusses the world's great blind writers and poets such as Homer, Milton and Borges. James Joyce ended his life almost blind following a series of unsuccessful cataract operations. One can add to the list, of course, other historical and contemporary blind writers, performers and professionals. According to Derrida, Milton, who became blind early in his career,

would have received blindness as a blessing, a prize, a reward, a divine 'requital', the gift of poetic and political clairvoyance, the chance for prophecy. There is nothing marvellous or astonishing in this: Marvell believed he knew that in losing his sight man does not lose his eyes. On the contrary. Only then does man begin to *think* the eyes (Derrida, 1993).

Derrida cites Marvell, a friend and contemporary of Milton, who believed this inner sight, this poetic vision, comes only through loss and suffering. This goes beyond metaphor to the primal core of the human body: the same eyes that see also weep, the same eyes that give us access to the outer world also, when blurred and weeping, transport us beyond vision into the heart of the event that so moves us.

It will come down to making a responsible choice for myself and for those individuals who are part of my immediate cultural world. I would become more dependent upon my family and society by letting my genes express themselves in the natural ageing of the corneas. I would have to give up some of my control and some of my expertise as a sighted person. I could no longer do many of the things by which self-sufficiency is defined in our culture. And how could I so easily forfeit the privilege of appreciating the beauty of the visual world and the opportunity to see for those who cannot?

In Utah, some of the biologists and ranchers view the blind horses as detrimental to the herd as a whole. The blind horses are less healthy and live shorter lives than the sighted horses. Some have proposed to euthanaze the blind horses, or capture them for adoption by humans, in order to selectively breed the blindness gene from the wild herd. Environmentalist Judy Cady, of the Colorado Wild Horse and Burro Coalition, is resisting these sentiments in favour of leaving the herd free.

Sure some are skinny but they have developed a unique way of getting around in a difficult environment. It's amazing that they find another horse and follow it around (Law, 1995).

References

Bruner, J. (1986). *Actual Minds, Possible Worlds.* Cambridge, MA: Harvard University Press.

Buber, M. (1992). *On Intersubjectivity and Cultural Creativity.* Chicago: University of Chicago Press.

Derrida, J. (1993). *Memoirs of the Blind: The self-portrait and other ruins.* (Transl P. Brault and M. Naas) Chicago: University of Chicago Press.

Fogel, A. (1993). *Developing through Relationships.* London: Harvester-Wheatsheaf.

Fogel, A. (1996). Information, creativity, and culture. In C. Dent-Read and P. Zukow-Goldring (Eds), *Changing Ecological Approaches to Development: Organism-environment mutualities.* Washington, DC: APA Publications.

Fraiberg, S. (1977). *Insights from the Blind.* New York: Basic Books.

Franco, F., Fogel, A., Messinger, D. S., and Frazier, C. A. (1996). Cultural differences in physical contact between Hispanic and Anglo mother–infant dyads living in the United States. *Early Development and Parenting, 5,* 119–127.

Galati, D. and Cattaneo, M. T. (1995). Vita quotidiana ed emozioni in soggetti con disabilita visiva (Everyday life and emotions in the visually impaired). *Richerche di Psicologia, 1,* 27–56.

Gibson, E. J. (1993). Ontogenesis of the perceived self. In U. Neisser (Ed.), *The Perceived Self.* New York: Cambridge University Press.

Gregory, R. L. (1966). *Eye and Brain: The psychology of seeing.* NY: World University Library.

Hatwell, Y. (1994). Elaborazione dei dati spaziali e sviluppo cognitivo dei non vedenti (Elaboration of spatial information and cognitive development in the blind). In D. Galati (Ed.), *Vedere con la Mente: Conoscenza, affettivita, adattamento nei non vedenti.* Milan: FrancoAngeli.

Johnson, M. (1987). *The Body in the Mind.* Chicago: University of Chicago Press.

Keller, H. (1908). *The World I Live In.* New York: The Century Company.

Law, S. (1995). Wild horses are blind. *Salt Lake Tribune, August.* Salt Lake City, Utah.

Masini, R. and Antonietti, A. (1994). Processi percettivi e rappresentativi nei non vedenti (Perceptual and representational processes in the blind). In D. Galati (Ed.), *Vedere con la Mente: Conoscenza, affettivita, adattamento nei non vedenti.* Milan: Franco Angeli.

Sachs, O. (1993). To see and not to see. *New Yorker,* May 10, 59–73.

Swan, J. (1992). Touching words: Helen Keller, plagiarism, authorship. Cardozo *Arts and Entertainment Law Journal, 10,* 321–364.

Swan, J. (1993). Blindness/deafness/narrative. Paper presented at the Humanities Center, University of Utah, March.

Truitt, A. (1982). *Daybook: The journal of an artist.* New York: Penguin Books.

Chapter Eight

'Autism' revisited: the case of congenital blindness

R. Peter Hobson, Rachel Brown, Margaret E. Minter and Anthony Lee

Consider the following clinical vignette:

At the age of four and a half years, Charles was brought to the clinic by his mother, who complained that 'the thing that upsets me most is that I can't reach my baby'. As a baby, this child would lie in the crib, just staring. When he was one and a half years old, he began to spend hours spinning toys and the lids of bottles and jars. His mother remarked, 'He would pay no attention to me and show no recognition of me if I entered the room . . . The most impressive thing is his detachment and his inaccessibility. He walks as if he is in a shadow, lives in a world of his own where he cannot be reached. No sense of relationship to persons. He went through a period of quoting another person; never offers anything himself. His entire conversation is a replica of whatever has been said to him. He used to speak of himself in the second person, now he uses the third person at times; he would say 'He wants' – never 'I want' . . . When he is with other people, he doesn't look up at them. Last July, we had a group of people. When Charles came in, it was just like a foal who'd been let out of an enclosure . . . He has a wonderful memory for words. Vocabulary is good, except for pronouns. He never initiates conversation, and conversation is limited, extensive only as far as objects go'.

Charles was one of Kanner's (1943) original cohort of 11 cases of *autistic disturbances of affective contact*; that is, he was a sighted child with the syndrome of early childhood autism. The enigma of autism is that it comprises a relatively consistent constellation of clinical features in seemingly disparate domains of human psychology: a marked lack of interpersonal engagement; an often profound and characteristic profile of abnormalities in language development (including difficulties with 'I' and 'you'); and a striking deficit in creative symbolic play, along with repetitive routines and interests. Why do these awesome and perplexing abnormalities co-occur in Kanner's syndrome? How can they be explained?

Consider a second vignette, concerning a child called Kathie.

When Kathie was two years old, her language competence compared favourably with that of a normal child of the same age. On the other hand, Kathie's confusions in personal pronoun use were unusually marked; 'Want me carry you?' she said to her mother when she herself wanted to be carried. Then between the ages of two and a half and three years, it became clear that Kathie could not represent herself through a toy or doll. She could not recreate or invent a situation in play. When tested at the age of just over three years, Kathie could neither pretend that playdough was a cookie, nor understand personal pronouns; when the interviewer asked 'Can I have a bite of the cookie, Kathie?', Kathie put the playdough in her own mouth and said 'This cookie different'. It was not until after she reached the age of four that Kathie began to represent herself in doll play, and in parallel with this, to master the use of personal pronouns.

Kathie was *not* autistic. By six years of age, she had become inventive in imaginative play, mischievous and fun-loving, independent and responsible as well as sociable and linguistically accomplished. Kathie was congenitally blind, one of the group of blind children studied by Fraiberg (1977).

So here is one socially able blind child whose problems in the areas of personal pronoun usage and symbolic play are more than a little reminiscent of those that characterize sighted autistic children. Are such clinical phenomena characteristic of blind children and, if so, why? And what about those blind children who are not socially able? It requires only a little experience of congenitally blind children, or a little reading of the literature about congenital blindness, to be struck by the remarkably severe social difficulties that many such children seem to manifest in the early and sometimes later years of their lives. Have these difficulties anything to do with autism? One can also observe ritualistic behaviour in some blind children, and perseverative tendencies in their thinking when language becomes more developed. And yet, there are plenty of blind children who seem to do remarkably well in overcoming what appears to be a potentially daunting perceptual handicap and develop much like their sighted peers. So what does all this mean?

In this chapter, the enigmatic condition of autism will be juxtaposed with the perplexing psychological difficulties of congenital blindness, in order to see whether two obscurities can clarify one another. In fact, the main objective is to clarify something about the nature of what is obscure about these conditions. There is a natural but regrettable tendency to think of autism as a *something* that an individual may have – the current terminology about 'persons with autism' reinforces this intellectual stance. The fact that autism is simply a descriptively based syndrome is too easily forgotten. Autism cannot be assumed to be the clinical manifestation of a relatively homogeneous neuropathological condition, nor (despite there being persuasive evidence from follow-up studies that severe disabilities tend to persist) can it be assumed that autism is a condition from which there is necessarily no escape. Rather, it is important to study and explain both the heterogeneity and the homogeneity to be observed in individuals who satisfy standard diagnostic criteria for childhood autism. And it is here that the study of special cases such as that of the blind autistic child may be especially revealing.

Now we experience some conflict at this point, in deciding how to proceed. If the aim is to present data on autism-like features in congenitally blind children, it seems perverse to put that off for a while in order to indulge in developmental theorizing. On the other hand, the studies to be discussed have arisen out of a theoretical debate commenced between one of us and two members of the Cognitive Development Unit, Alan Leslie and Uta Frith, in the pages of the *Psychological Review* a few years ago (Leslie, 1987; Hobson, 1990; Leslie and Frith, 1990). From one point of view, the investigations to be reported represent something of a test between competing theories, rather than a trawling exercise for clinical features in blind children. Moreover, the concern of other authors in this volume is even broader and more ambitious than meeting the challenge of understanding blind people's development – it is to deepen our understanding of *all* children's development through the study of those who are blind. In this chapter, that approach will be taken one step further by introducing early childhood autism as an additional illuminating and to-be-illuminated condition.

Two theories of mental development

First, two contemporary theories of early normal development and early childhood autism will be outlined. Then we shall suggest why the study of blind children may help to tip the balance towards one or other of the two rival viewpoints.

The critical point of similarity between the two theories – and here there is little space to draw contrasts with other kinds of theory – is that they posit an intrinsic relation between normal sighted children's early understanding of minds, and the emergence of creative symbolic play and context-sensitive language around the middle of the second year of life. Moreover, they each propose that early childhood autism is a disorder of development in which something has gone wrong with whatever links these seemingly disparate psychological abilities.

Leslie's approach (Leslie, 1987) was the earlier-appearing of the theories. He considers infants to begin with the capacity to form *primary representations* that encode aspects of the world in an accurate, faithful, and literal way. Towards the end of infancy, however, through the operation of an innately determined *decoupling mechanism*, children acquire the ability to represent not only the world, but also these representations themselves: it is as if children were quoting someone else, lifting out the representation, without committing themselves to the truth of whatever the person said or thought. The block of wood 'is' a car, the doll 'can' speak, and so on. In this way, they acquire the ability to engage in pretend symbolic play.

Leslie's thesis is that children's ability to recognize the nature of mental states in themselves and others depends on the same innately-derived cognitive capacity that underpins the ability to pretend. We say *innately derived* because Leslie's idea is that the decoupling mechanism simply comes online at a particular point in development. Leslie offered the hypothesis that autistic children have an absence or malfunction of the decoupling mechanism, and are thereby impaired in forming metarepresentations. He suggested this as an explanation for their impairments in symbolic play and for their 'specific deficit in theory of mind' (p.424; see also Leslie, 1991), including their difficulty in understanding how other people's behaviour depends upon their beliefs.

By positing this switching on of a new computational function at around 18 months of age, Leslie may have left out a great deal that is essential to children's early understanding of minds and to their acquisition of symbolic play and language. According to the second theoretical account (Hobson, 1993a), the decoupling mechanism is what needs to be explained, not merely described, and for this, the story must begin much earlier in infancy. The account starts with the fact that babies experience an *intersubjective connectedness* with, and at times disconnectedness from, other persons (Trevarthen, 1979). It is posited that, through patterned interpersonal affective co-ordination, and the infant's capacity to register in his or her own feelings the emotional attitudes of others (especially, when another person is relating to him or herself), the infant comes to understand what it means to share experiences, and ultimately, what it means for others to have their own psychological states that are both similar to, yet distinct from, the infant's own.

Then towards the end of the first year of life, and before understanding much about persons, infants register and react to the *directedness* of other people's attitudes and actions towards a shared world. Imagine a 12-month-old perceiving another person to have a particular attitude towards some object on which the child's attention is focused, or the infant perceiving a person performing an action on something. Now suppose the infant identifies with the attitude or action manifest in the other person's bodily expressions or movements, so that the infant comes to assume the other's psychological stance. If it were the case that the infant came to understand his or her new psychological orientation to be a new and separate psychological orientation, and moreover one that was 'about' something other than himself or herself, such movement to another person's mental stance would constitute a movement in thought.

According to this account, an infant's emotional reactions to and appropriation of other people's attitudes towards the world are critical for disembedding the infant from an immediate, unreflective and concrete apprehension of the environment. The reason is that they constitute the route by which the infant comes to adopt, and, in due course, to recognize, multiple attitudes to the same things and events. If the same things can be the objects of different attitudes, then things are different from thoughts. With insight into this, the child can knowingly confer novel attitudes (thoughts) onto familiar things in symbolic play, and can appreciate how she or he, as well as others, can capture and intentionally convey attitudes and thoughts in language. In other words, it is through an infant's experiences of his or her own attitudes to, and with other people's attitudes to, a visually-specified world, that he or she comes to appreciate two complementary facts of psychological life: objects can have multiple meanings-for-persons, and persons can hold multiple attitudes to given objects. Moreover, as Mead (1934) described, significant symbols arise in conjunction with self-reflective awareness when the child takes the role of the other *vis-à-vis* itself.

Now if all this is the case, then it is possible to consider whether there are conditions in which children are restricted in perceiving the relation between people's attitudes and the objects and events in the world toward which those attitudes are directed. Autistic children appear to face difficulty in perceiving, responding to, and identifying with, attitudes *as* attitudes. They can see the directedness of actions, for example, but their affective engagement with the emotional attitudes of others is seriously impaired. But suppose there are children whose problem is not so much in having an impaired affective response to other people, but rather in perceiving how other people's attitudes are *directed* at a world which is also the world experienced by the child him or herself. This, too, would deprive such a child of the kinds of social triangulation which, it is suggested, are the basis for symbolic thinking, self-reflective awareness, and context-sensitive language and thought. It is for this reason that it is relevant to study blind children for, if this is a condition in which an autistic-like syndrome is the developmental outcome of a handicap which is not a missing cognitive decoupling mechanism, then an account which focuses on obstacles to achieving normal patterns of interpersonal relatedness might be the explanation of choice. And it is clear that blind children cannot *see* how people's attitudes are directed to a visually specified and shared external world. The thesis is that because of this, they have that much more difficulty in triangulating self, other, and the objects towards which attitudes are directed, and therefore more difficulty in recognizing how meanings are person-dependent and ascribable in symbolic play.

So much for the theoretical background, except for one further matter. Although contrasts between the two developmental theories have been highlighted, it is important to acknowledge that, in a number of ways, they are very similar. In particular, they each posit that a syndrome comprising a variety of impairments in interpersonal understanding, and in flexible symbolic functioning and language, arises as the developmental outcome of a single psychological deficit. For one account this deficit is cognitive, whilst for the other it lies in severe disruption (which may be of various kinds) in patterned intersubjective communication and identification between a child and others. It should be emphasized that neither of these accounts suggests that autism or autistic-like phenomena are psychogenic, because each allows that neurological dysfunction (which may be caused by a variety of medical conditions) is usually if not always necessary, and quite possibly sufficient, to cause autism, at least in sighted children. So, too, brain damage that is coincidental with blindness may play an important role in leading to autism in blind children. The point to stress is that there are a number of theories in which a range of different autistic-like phenomena are supposed to arise more or less directly out of different forms of neuropsychological deficit. For example, some researchers are exploring whether autistic children's perseverative tendencies and lack of flexibility may result from primary dysfunction in executive function, as mediated by the fronto-limbic system (for example, Ozonoff, Strayer, McMahon and Filloux, 1994). If this is the case, then only certain facets of the clinical picture will require explanation in specifically developmental terms. This needs to be borne in mind when considering the potential implications of blind children's lack of visual experience. The perceptual handicap may be neither necessary nor sufficient for the children's psychological abnormalities, or it may only be important when acting in concert with other factors that interfere with normal development, whether these are organic or environmental in nature.

Autism and autistic-like features in blind children

There are numerous reports in the literature of visually impaired children who have the syndrome of autism or who manifest autistic features. The clinical vignette of the blind child Kathie, described earlier, was taken from the writings of Fraiberg (1977), who provided vivid descriptions of such children. Fraiberg was convinced that autism in the blind child is not associated with any specific ophthal- mological disease, and she considered that the seven autistic out of 27 blind children referred to herself and colleagues when she worked in New Orleans 'fairly represented the incidence of autism in the blind population' (Fraiberg 1977, p.4). Although clinical-descriptive accounts fill out the picture of autistic-like syndromes in blind children (for example, Blank, 1975; Curson, 1979; Elonen and Cain, 1964; Green and Schecter, 1957; McGuire, 1969; Wills, 1981), other workers dealing with heterogeneous groups of partially sighted and blind children have been less impressed by the prevalence of the syn- drome (Jan, Freeman and Scott, 1977; Norris, Spaulding and Brodie, 1957). However, intensive study of congenitally severely visually impaired children with conditions such as retrolental fibroplasia (Chase, 1972; Keeler, 1958), rubella (Chess, 1971; Wing, 1969) and Leber's amaurosis (Rogers and Newhart-Larson, 1989) have con- firmed that the syndrome is relatively common in at least certain subgroups of blind children.

Much more widespread among blind children are so-called autistic features such as stereotypies and ritualistic behaviour (Jan *et al.*, 1977; Sandler, 1963; Wills, 1979), echolalia and confusions in personal pro- noun usage (Andersen, Dunlea and Kekelis, 1984; Fay, 1973; Fraiberg, 1977; McGuire, 1969) and abnormalities in social communicative competence (Fraiberg, 1977; Preisler, 1993; Rowland, 1983; Tröster and Brambring, 1992). There is also some evidence that blind children may have delays in developing creative symbolic play (Fraiberg, 1977; Preisler, 1993; Rogers and Puchalski, 1984; Wills, 1981), have specific difficulty in recognizing vocally expressed emotions (Minter, Hobson and Pring, 1991), and encounter particular problems with abstract thinking (Tillman, 1967; Warren, 1977; Wills, 1981). It begs important questions, of course, to call such clinical features and psychological abnormalities autistic-like. Are they simply reminiscent of what one observes in sighted autistic children, or are they truly similar in patho- genesis, in form, and in natural history? Is there a gradient in the number and severity of autistic-like features in blind children, for example as Chase (1972) reported in a group with retrolental fibro- plasia, or is there a clear distinction between blind children with one or two such features and others who have the full syndrome of autism? Whatever the answers to these questions, how are we to understand the origins and nature of the clinical phenomena?

The following study (described more fully in Brown, Hobson, Lee and Stevenson, in press) provides evidence that is relevant for address- ing these issues, although it does not resolve them.

A clinical–observational study of congenitally blind, autistic and mainstream sighted children

The aim of this study was to determine whether it is the case that 'autistic-like' clinical features are common in congenitally blind children, and to examine whether blind children who present with the syndrome of autism are indeed similar to sighted autistic children of similar age and verbal ability.

Twenty-four children were selected from six schools for the blind, on the basis that they were aged between three and nine years of age, had suffered total blindness or only minimal light perception from birth, were testable, and had no identifiable neurological impairment. The sample was restricted to congenitally blind children, for the reason that even relatively brief periods of sight early in life, or even moderate degrees of vision, often appear to make a considerable difference to visually impaired children's development. All children were tested for verbal IQ on versions of the *Wechsler Pre-School and Primary Scale of Intelligence (WIPPSI)* or the *Wechsler Intelligence Scale for Children–Revised (WISC–R)* which did not include pictorial testing material (Wechsler, 1967; Wechsler, 1976).

The 24 blind children were divided into two groups: those with an IQ above 70, and those with an IQ less than 70. Subsequently, the data were re-analysed after dividing the blind children into those who were most like sighted children with autism, and the remainder. In fact, the large majority of the autistic-like blind children fell into the low-IQ group, and the findings to be reported were not altered by these minor adjustments in group composition. The upper-ability group of 15 blind children was compared with 10 sighted children from mainstream schools who were group-matched for age and verbal ability; the mean chronological age (CA) and verbal mental age (MA) of the children of each group was approximately six years. The lower-ability group of nine blind children was compared with nine sighted autistic children who were group matched for verbal ability and approximately for age; for the blind children, mean CA = six years, seven months; MA = three years, ten months; for the sighted autistic children, mean CA = eight years, six months; MA = three years, nine months.

Each of the children was observed for at least three periods of 20 minutes in different settings: at free play; in the classroom during a lesson; and in a session of language testing. On the basis of these observations, two standardized rating schedules were completed. The first was the *Childhood Autism Rating Scale (CARS)* (Schopler, Reichler and Renner, 1988), which contains 15 items scored from one to four, with a score of one indicating age-appropriate behaviour and a score of four representing severely abnormal behaviour. Items include such characteristics as relationships with people, nonverbal communication, adaptation to change, and affect. The second measure was the *Behavior Checklist for Disordered Preschoolers (BCDP)* by Sherman, Shapiro and Glassman (1983). This contains 29 items concerned with relatedness to other people (for example, responses to active attempts at engagement by other people, nature of physical contact and interactive play), relatedness to the physical surroundings (for example, attitude towards presented objects, and perseveration), motor disturbances (for example, postural oddities and motor stereotypies) and language impairment (such as vocabulary size, immediate echolalia and context-appropriate speech).

In addition, each child was discussed with a teacher who knew the child well, focusing upon items on a checklist abstracted from the *DSM-III-R* criteria for autism, and eliciting examples of each positive clinical feature. At the conclusion of the study, the investigator (a child psychiatrist with considerable experience of developmental disorders) also reflected upon her own observations of and contact with each of the children, and considered whether she would have given them a diagnosis of childhood autism.

The congenitally blind sample

It is appropriate to make some preliminary observations about the group of 24 congenitally blind children. Twenty-one of these children had total blindness, and three had minimal light perception. There were a range of medical diagnoses, fairly evenly spread across the upper- and lower-IQ groups; there were 12 children with retinopathy of prematurity, five with optic atrophy, three with Leber's amaurosis, two with Norris's disease, and two with other disorders of the visual system.

The first issue concerned the distribution of autistic-like features across the group of blind children. As already described, the 15 items on the *CARS* are each indicative of a potentially autistic-like clinical feature, and mainstream children (including every one of the mainstream children in the study) generally score 15, the minimum score. Although any deviation from this is unusual, children with scores lower than 30 are conventionally characterized as non-autistic, although this is not a rigid criterion. One of the items (Item VII) concerns visual responsiveness, and this was excluded from the observations (thereby reducing the maximum achievable score by four).

The distribution of *CARS* scores is shown in *Figure 8.1*. This reveals that there were no blind children with the minimum score, a relatively large proportion (over 50 per cent) with a somewhat elevated score, and the remainder with a range of scores extending into the autistic domain. Although one might consider this a bimodal distribution of scores, there is no clear separation between low-scoring and high-scoring children: it appears that there is a continuum in the numbers and severity of autistic-like clinical features in congenitally blind children.

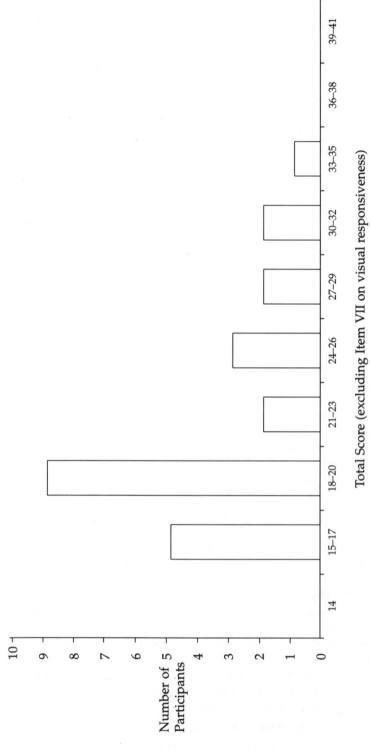

Figure 8.1. Distribution of blind children's scores on the Childhood Autism Rating Scale.

Having stated this, it is also revealing to consider how many of the congenitally blind children satisfied the DSM-III-R criteria for autism, according to the checklist. For this diagnosis, a categorical judgement, a child needs to show at least one clinical feature under the heading 'impairment in communication', two abnormalities in reciprocal social interaction, and one manifestation of restricted activities, interests and imagination. In the event, 10 out of the 24 congenitally blind children satisfied these criteria, a proportion that is strikingly similar to the seven out of 27 which Fraiberg (1977) considered to represent the incidence of autism in the population of blind children. This diagnosis was not restricted to any particular medical diagnosis.

The fifteen upper-ability blind children compared with the ten mainstream sighted children

In this study, there were multiple observations made on a small number of subjects. In order to manage the data, therefore, the CARS and BCDP measures were factor analyzed, and a principal component analysis was conducted to identify the main dimensions accounting for the item scores within these scales. There was one factor of the CARS ('social impairment') that accounted for a substantial proportion of the variance (54%), and a somewhat similar factor on the BCDP (accounting for 36% of the variance). A MANOVA revealed that for each of these factors, the group means were significantly different. When individual items were examined, there were significant differences in a variety of respects, including relating to people, body use, response to objects, verbal and non-verbal communication, motor co-ordination, interactive play and type of play activity, and immediate echolalia.

The nine lower ability blind children compared with the nine sighted autistic children

In this comparison, there were no significant differences between the mean factor scores of the blind and sighted autistic children. Therefore an analysis of individual items on the scales was not justified. On visual inspection of the results from the CARS, BCDP and DSM-III-R checklist, the similarities between the groups were far more striking that the differences. However, it was also noted that if one considered only the more severe manifestations of each of the CARS categories, a clear majority of the sighted autistic children but only a small minority of the blind children were rated as having such profound abnormalities in relating to people, in their emotional responses, and especially in their degree of autism according to 'general impressions'.

This latter observation must be treated with circumspection, of course, in that it represents a *post hoc* selection of data from a large number of group comparisons. On the other hand, it accords with the clinician's diagnostic judgement of the children (a judgement that was not independent of the observational ratings, since the same individual was involved in each evaluation): she considered that she could be confident of the diagnosis of Kanner-type autism in only two of the congenitally blind children, in that the quality of the other blind children's social impairment, and specifically the quality of affective engagement and communication with others, was not quite the same as that in the sighted autistic individuals.

Theory of mind in children with visual impairment

In the early, theoretical part of this chapter, two theories were presented in which psychological abilities related to interpersonal understanding (theory of mind) were supposed to be important for a number of seemingly disparate domains of children's intellectual and language ability. Correspondingly, certain of the phenomena of early childhood autism were taken to reflect impairment in such understanding. The question arises whether blind children are like sighted autistic children in having specific delays and/or limitations in theory of mind understanding.

At present there is little evidence on this topic, but some recent studies are highly suggestive. McAlpine and Moore (1995) conducted an uncontrolled study in which they adapted a task from Perner, Leekam and Wimmer (1987) to test whether visually impaired children could predict what someone would expect to find in a familiar container (one for a hamburger, the other for milk) when the participants themselves knew these actually contained a sock and water, respectively. The children were aged between four and 12 years, and almost all were above average intelligence on formal testing. Whereas eight out of nine of the children with visual acuity of 20/240 or above responded correctly on both versions of the theory of mind task, only two out of seven children with more severe visual impairment did so, even though their mental ages were 4 years 6 months or above, a level at which sighted children might be expected to respond correctly.

Recently, we have completed a controlled study of non-autistic congenitally blind children in which we have employed two rather different tasks (Minter, Hobson and Bishop, in press). The first was also modelled on that of Perner et al. (1987), but took the form of asking 21 blind and 21 matched sighted children aged between 5 and 9 years (mean verbal mental age of each group 6 years 10 months) to feel a warm teapot and to guess its contents. They were then shown that it contained sand, not liquid. The children were asked two questions, in counterbalanced order: what they first thought was in the teapot, before the contents were poured out (the *representational change* question), and what a peer who was coming in next would think was in the teapot when he/she felt it. The results were that nearly all the sighted children answered both questions correctly, but approximately half the blind children answered one or both of the questions incorrectly, basing their replies on their current awareness of the teapot's contents.

In a subsequent task based on the method of Wimmer and Perner (1983), but employing a method that depended on touch, children were asked to predict in which box a person would look for a pencil when, in the person's prior absence, the pencil was moved from one kind of box and hidden in another kind of box. In this case, all the sighted and also the majority of the blind children made a correct prediction, but a significant minority (20%) of the blind children failed to do so.

What struck us when conducting this task, was how careful we had to be in communicating to the blind children through language and touch, what we were asking about. At times it was also difficult to interpret their responses, and we had to set a number of responses aside from the main data because they were ambiguous. Therefore one needs to be cautious about concluding that some blind children lack concepts of belief and so on. On the other hand, this study has revealed just the kinds of difficulty in psychological co-reference between the children and others that may be significant for the development of theory of mind and related abilities. Moreover, it proved to be the case that a number of congenitally blind children were impaired in evaluating the beliefs and expectations of others.

Conclusions

Hopefully, this chapter has persuaded readers that there is something interesting and important to understand about the common ground that exists between congenitally blind children and sighted autistic children, as regards their early psychological development. Many congenitally blind children show 'autistic-like' features – so many, in fact, that one might even wonder whether there is a case for thinking of certain of the phenomena of autism as 'congenitally-blind-like'! Although the children studied were not, of course, an epidemiological sample, and the study may have overestimated the prevalence of severe psychological disorders in congenitally blind children, a substantial number of such children have a constellation of clinical features that amounts to, or is very like, the syndrome of autism. On the other hand, there was some suggestive evidence that the quality of blind children's social-communicative impairment was not typical of autism in sighted children, raising the possibility that lack of visual experience *per se* might act in concert with other factors in giving rise to the syndrome. There was also preliminary evidence that even non-autistic congenitally blind children may have difficulties on tasks that require sensitivity to other people's psychological orientations and beliefs, a matter that may be relevant to understanding certain of the children's autistic-like features, such as echolalia and creative symbolic play (Andersen *et al.*, 1984; Hobson, 1993b).

There are two issues that deserve a final comment. First, although the studies described do not provide decisive evidence in relation to the theoretical debate about the developmental psychopathology of autism, they do suggest that psychological impairments related to those of sighted autistic children may occur in congenitally blind children, sometimes with and sometimes without the full syndrome. This finding raises questions about whether autism could be explained by an autism-specific cognitive deficit. It might incline one instead towards a social-developmental account of certain autistic-like phenomena, whether these occur in sighted or congenitally blind children, and perhaps even suggest a perceptual-developmental account of a range of autistic-like features (for example, Wing, 1969). Second, it is important to recognize the uncertainty that remains about the role of cognitive and/or social-communicative factors in the pathogenesis of autism and autistic-like features in congenitally blind children. As Keeler (1958) reflected with regard to his cases of autistic-like children with retrolental fibroplasia many years ago, the clinical picture of autism may arise as the result of a complex of factors including total or near total blindness from birth, brain damage, and possibly in some cases such as those involving institutionalization, inadequate or insufficiently sensitive environmental provision (Blank, 1975; Cass, Sonksen and McConachie, 1994; Fraiberg, 1977; Goodyear, Sonksen, and McConachie, 1989). There is much to discover about the psychological development of congenitally blind children and about that of sighted autistic children, and there is a real possibility that each of these conditions may further our understanding of the other.

Acknowledgement

Jim Stevenson and Martin Bishop provided invaluable collaboration for aspects of these studies. We are very grateful to the children who allowed us to study them, and for the patience and generosity of their teachers.

References

Andersen, E. S., Dunlea, A. and Kekelis, L. S. (1984). Blind children's language: resolving some differences. *Journal of Child Language, 11*, 645–664.
Blank, H. R. (1975). Reflections on the special senses in relation to the development of affect with special emphasis on blindness. *Journal of the American Psychoanalytic Association, 23*, 32–50.

Brown, R., Hobson R. P., Lee, A. and Stevenson, J. (in press). Are there 'autistic-like' features in congenitally blind children? *Journal of Child Psychology and Psychiatry.*

Cass, H. D., Sonksen, P. M. and McConachie, H. R. (1994). Developmental setback in severe visual impairment. *Archives of Disease in Childhood, 70,* 192–196.

Chase, J. B. (1972). *Retrolental Fibroplasia and Autistic Symptomatology.* New York: American Foundation for the Blind.

Chess, S. (1971). Autism in children with congenital rubella. *Journal of Autism and Childhood Schizophrenia, 1,* 33–47.

Curson, A. (1979). The blind nursery school child. *Psychoanalytic Study of the Child, 34,* 51–83.

Elonen, A. S. and Cain, A. C. (1964). Diagnostic evaluation and treatment of deviant blind children. *American Journal of Orthopsychiatry, 34,* 625–633.

Fay, W. H. (1973). On the echolalia of the blind and the autistic child. *Journal of Speech and Hearing Disorders, 38,* 478–489.

Fraiberg, S. (1977). *Insights from the Blind.* London: Souvenir.

Goodyear, H. M., Sonksen, P.M. and McConachie, H. (1989). Norrie's disease: a prospective study of development. *Archives of Disease in Childhood, 64,* 1587–1592.

Green, M. R. and Schecter, D. E. (1957). Autistic and symbiotic disorders in three blind children. *Psychiatric Quarterly, 31,* 628–646.

Hobson, R. P. (1990). On acquiring knowledge about people and the capacity to pretend: A response to Leslie. *Psychological Review, 97,* 114–121.

Hobson, R. P. (1993a). Through feeling and sight to self and symbol. In U. Neisser (Ed.), *The Perceived Self: Ecological and interpersonal knowledge of self.* Cambridge: Cambridge University Press.

Hobson, R. P. (1993b). *Autism and the Development of Mind.* Hove, Sussex: Lawrence Erlbaum.

Jan, J. E., Freeman, R. D. and Scott, E. P. (1977). *Visual Impairment in Children and Adolescents.* New York: Grune and Stratton.

Kanner, L. (1943). Autistic disturbances of affective contact. *Nervous Child, 2,* 217–250.

Keeler, W. R. (1958). Autistic patterns and defective communication in blind children with retrolental fibroplasia. In P. H. Hoch and J. Zubin (Eds), *Psychopathology of Communication.* New York: Grune and Stratton.

Leslie, A.M. (1987). Pretense and representation: the origins of 'theory of mind'. *Psychological Review, 94,* 412–426.

Leslie, A.M. (1991). The theory of mind impairment in autism: evidence for a modular mechanism of development? In A. Whiten (Ed.), *Natural Theories of Mind.* Oxford: Blackwell

Leslie, A.M. and Frith, U. (1990). Prospects for a cognitive neuropsychology of autism: Hobson's choice. *Psychological Review, 97,* 122–131.

McAlpine, L. M. and Moore, C. (1995). The development of social understanding in children with visual impairments. *Journal of Visual Impairment and Blindness, 89,* 349–358.

McGuire, L. L. (1969). *Psycho-dynamic Development Problems in the Congenitally Blind*. Los Angeles: University of Southern California.

Mead, G. H. (1934). *Mind, Self and Society*. Chicago: University of Chicago Press.

Minter, M., Hobson R. P., and Bishop, M. (in press) Congenital visual impairment and 'theory of mind'. *British Journal of Developmental Psychology*.

Minter, M. E., Hobson, R. P., and Pring, L. (1991). Recognition of vocally expressed emotion by congenitally blind children. *Journal of Visual Impairment and Blindness, 85,* 411–415.

Norris, M., Spaulding, P. J. and Brodie, F. H. (1957). *Blindness in Children*. Chicago: University of Chicago Press.

Ozonoff, S., Strayer, D. L., McMahon, W. M., and Filloux, F. (1994). Executive function abilities in autism and Tourette syndrome: an information processing approach. *Journal of Child Psychology and Psychiatry and Allied Disciplines, 35,* 1015–1032.

Perner, J., Leekam, S. R., and Wimmer, H. (1987). Three-year-olds' difficulty with false belief: the case for a conceptual deficit. *British Journal of Developmental Psychology, 5,* 125–137.

Preisler, G. M. (1993). A descriptive study of blind children in nurseries with sighted children. *Child: care, health and development, 19,* 295–315.

Rogers, S. J. and Newhart-Larson, S. (1989). Characteristics of infantile autism in five children with Leber's congenital amaurosis. *Developmental Medicine and Child Neurology, 31,* 598–608.

Rogers, S. J. and Puchalski, C. B. (1984). Development of symbolic play in visually impaired young children. *Topics in Early Childhood Special Education, 3,* 57–63.

Rowland, C. (1983). Patterns of interaction between three blind infants and their mothers. In A. E. Mills (Ed.), *Language Acquisition in the Blind Child: Normal and deficient*. London: Croom Helm

Sandler, A-M. (1963). Aspects of passivity and ego development in the blind infant. *Psychoanalytic Study of the Child, 28,* 343–360.

Schopler, E., Reichler, R. J. and Renner, B. R. (1988). *The Childhood Autism Rating Scale (CARS)*. Los Angeles, CA: Western Psychological Services.

Sherman, M., Shapiro, T., and Glassman, M. (1983). Play and language in developmentally disordered preschoolers: A new approach to classification. *Journal of the American Academy of Child Psychiatry, 22,* 511–524.

Tillman, M. H. (1967). The performance of blind and sighted children on the Wechsler Intelligence Scale for Children: Study II. *International Journal for the Education of the Blind, 16,* 106–112.

Trevarthen, C. (1979). Communication and co-operation in early infancy: A description of primary intersubjectivity. In M. Bullowa (Ed.), *Before Speech*. Cambridge: Cambridge University Press.

Tröster, H. and Brambring, M. (1992). Early social-emotional development in blind infants. *Child: care, health and development, 18,* 207–227.

Warren, D. H. (1977). *Blindness and Early Childhood Development*. New York: American Foundation for the Blind.

Wechsler, D. (1967). *Wechsler Preschool and Primary Scale of Intelligence.* Cleveland, Ohio: Psychological Corporation.

Wechsler, D. (1976). *The Wechsler Intelligence Scale for Children–Revised.* Sidcup: Psychological Corporation.

Wills, D. M. (1979). Early speech development in blind children. *Psychoanalytic Study of the Child, 34,* 85–117.

Wills, D. M. (1981). Some notes on the application of the diagnostic profile to young blind children. *Psychoanalytic Study of the Child, 36,* 217–237.

Wimmer, H. and Perner, J. (1983). Beliefs about beliefs: representation and constraining function of wrong beliefs in young children's understanding of deception. *Cognition, 13,* 103–128.

Wing, L. (1969). The handicaps of autistic children – A comparative study. *Journal of Child Psychology and Psychiatry and Allied Disciplines, 10,* 1–40.

Chapter Nine

Establishing intersubjective experience: developmental challenges for young children with congenital blindness and autism and their caregivers

Susan L. Recchia

Intersubjectivity, a synchronized attention to, and understanding of, events and emotions, is so much a part of the typical experience of young children and their caregivers that it is often taken for granted. Viewed as foundational to other developing competences such as language and social cognition, intersubjective experience begins early in the first year of life and continues to be refined as children, and their relationships, mature and become more complex. Researchers have reported clinical observations of behavioural indices of intersubjective experience, such as joint visual attention, joint referencing, and social referencing, and measured them within experimental paradigms (Bruner, 1977; Campos and Stenberg, 1981; Klinnert, Campos, Sorce, Emde and Svejda, 1983; Stern, 1985). Some view the establishment of these early social experiences as an important milestone in the development of social and emotional communication, and adaptive for species development (Campos and Stenberg, 1981).

In normally developing infants, intersubjective experience such as that observed in joint attention and social referencing, is viewed as a spontaneous development, evolving out of the natural context of routine child–caregiver interactions. Infants' sensory, motor, and perceptual competencies, and caregivers' sensitivity and responsiveness are the basic ingredients to the experience of intersubjectivity, and are assumed to be in place. Experimental observations of intersubjective experience focus largely on visual demonstrations of attention in young children, and caregivers are often assessed for their non-verbal expressions and communications (Recchia, 1993). In a typical social referencing paradigm, for example, children look to their mothers for cues in their facial expressions, and respond themselves as a function of their mothers' responses (Klinnert, 1984; Hornik, Risenhoover and Gunnar, 1987).

The presumed importance of intersubjective experience to later developmental competences makes it an especially interesting capacity to study in children who are at risk for delays or developmental differences in social cognition and communication. Two such populations discussed in the recent literature are the congenitally blind, and children with autism. When infants' sensory and perceptual systems suffer the impact of developmental delays or disabilities, the development of intersubjectivity may not follow its usual course (Fraiberg, 1977; Mulford, 1983; Frith and Baron-Cohen, 1987; Kopp and Recchia, 1990; Hobson, 1993; Lord, 1993; Warren, 1994; Recchia, in press). Caregivers' responses to children may also be different than expected when their primary means of fostering exploration and learning do not match their children's primary modes of accessing information (McGurk, 1983; Kekelis and Andersen, 1984; Lewis, 1987; Provence and Dahl, 1987; Moore and McConachie, 1994).

Observations of developmental processes in atypical populations inform our understanding of both the impact of disability on a particular capacity, and the role of intact competences in the development of that capacity. Researchers have questioned the origins of deficits in the development of intersubjectivity in infants and toddlers who are blind or autistic, and have explored the nature of similarities and differences between these different populations (Rogers and Newhart-Larson, 1989; Hobson, this volume; Preisler, this volume). In several recent investigations, experimental paradigms have been designed to elicit measurable aspects of intersubjectivity in both autistic (Sigman, Mundy, Sherman and Ungerer, 1986) and congenitally blind children (Recchia, 1993). Although some striking similarities have been observed in these two populations, both conceptual and qualitative differences in their behaviours, as well as the capacity for change in these behaviours over time, have posed interesting questions for future research. Questions also remain about the effectiveness of intervention strategies for these two similar, yet different, populations.

This chapter is, in part, a response to the interesting questions posed by Hobson et al. (Chapter 9) about the nature of autistic-like behaviour in congenitally blind children, and the degree to which each of these populations can inform our understanding of the other. It also reflects my own clinical experience of intervention with children with severe visual impairments and their families, as well as recent research with this population (Recchia, 1986; 1987; 1993; 1996; in press). My goals are to explore the development of intersubjective experience in congenitally blind children, and the similarities and differences between children with congenital blindness and autism in this respect. The focus will be on: similarities in the characteristics of conceptual functioning of these two populations of children which place them at risk for delays or deviations in the development of intersubjectivity; the significance of caregiver contributions to intersubjective experience, and the impact of the disabilities on relationships with caregivers; and differences in developmental adaptations and expected outcomes for the populations. The chapter concludes with suggestions for future research with both populations of young children.

One point of clarification should be made at the start. In discussing children with congenital blindness and autism, the focus will be on the underlying psychological implications of these disabilities. Because both of these populations are highly diverse, particular comments may be less applicable to some of the many children within both diagnostic areas who present with multiple impairments. As it is impossible to cleanly separate the effects of additional impairments on children's functioning, this will not be attempted.

Similarities in the early intersubjective experience of children with autism and congenital blindness

Hobson *et al.* (Chapter 9) have argued convincingly that the young autistic child's deficit in symbolic understanding is not simply cognitive, but social in nature. They discuss the ways in which children's perceptions of the relationship between attitudes and objects pose problems for both autistic and blind children, but for different reasons. While congenitally blind children are unable to see visual evidence of their partner's attitudes, autistic children appear unable to take in or process this information. Despite differences in the nature of the children's sensory and perceptual processes, however, both populations may be similarly challenged, at least initially, in their ability to come to an integrated understanding of the meaning of many social events.

Although both groups are highly heterogeneous, there appears to be a greater distinction in the quality of social behaviour between lower and higher functioning blind children. Blind children also demonstrate a greater range of social ability, and, unlike autistic populations (Volkmar, Burack and Cohen, 1990), older populations of blind children include some who are socially normal. However, the incidence of autistic-like features in both younger and older children with severe visual impairments is significant enough to merit attention (Fraiberg,

1977; Hobson, this volume). Exploring the ways in which early experiences within these two populations may overlap raises interesting questions about the cognitive and environmental contributions to the process of intersubjectivity, and the capacity for adaptation in children and their caregivers (Kopp and Recchia, 1990).

Cognition, perceptual understanding, and social responsiveness

Explanations for deviations in autistic children's social development focus on both cognitive and perceptual understandings (Frith and Baron-Cohen, 1987; Sigman, Ungerer, Mundy and Sherman, 1987; Volkmar, 1987). Both areas are implicated in how stimuli are interpreted, and subsequently responded to. Overly high levels of arousal may result in children either excluding pertinent information or attending to unusual stimuli, making it extremely difficult for their caregivers to discover what they know and understand (Lord, 1993).

Sigman and her colleagues (Sigman *et al.*, 1987) suggest that social learning may require a level of cognitive functioning that goes beyond the information processing capacity of the autistic child. They describe the young autistic child as unable to integrate emotion and attention in meaningful ways, and consequently being at a loss in interpreting communicative gestures and facial expressions. Lord (1993) suggests that there may be further difficulty in co-ordinating verbal and non-verbal behaviour. Thus, young autistic children are challenged by two aspects of social development important to intersubjectivity: anticipating the social behaviour of others, and adapting their own behaviour in response to others.

Differences in cognitive and perceptual understanding have also been reported for blind children (Fraiberg, 1977). In the absence of vision, children are slower to develop cognitive schemes that can be used to interpret new tactual and auditory experiences (Warren, 1984). The role that vision plays as an organizer of experience for sighted children has no ready substitute in children with severe visual impairments.

Limitations imposed by decreased sensory access can result in the congenitally blind child having restricted experience in the construction of reality (Sostek, 1991; Recchia, in press). Landau (1991) discusses the impoverished nature of aural relative to visual information, and the ways in which this has an impact on the young blind child's ability to demonstrate knowledge. In the absence of vision, access to non-auditory information which contributes meaningfully to social context is severely limited. Mutually constructed social experience such as that shared in intersubjectivity, if it occurs at all, will require adaptations on the part of both child and caregiver. Verbal and non-verbal behavioural matching cannot be learned incidentally. The degree to which non-verbal expression underlies social communication may affect the child's processing ability and ultimate situational understanding of an event.

Different constructions, common experience?

Although the nature and the origins of the cognitive and perceptual deviations experienced by blind and autistic children differ, various similarities in their behaviour have led researchers to question whether they share a similar deficit in social-cognitive understanding (for example, Hobson, 1993). Indeed, behavioural demonstrations made evident in toddlers' and pre-schoolers' language and play, such as the use of echolalia, confusion in the usage of personal pronouns and deictic terms, stereotypies and ritualistic behaviour, may contribute to the continued challenges to establishing intersubjectivity for both populations of children. However, for some congenitally blind children who are neurologically intact, there is evidence that growth in symbolic understanding comes about with increased appropriate language and exploratory experience (Hobson, 1993; Warren, 1994). Despite early developmental delays, many of these children will demonstrate functional academic and social skills by middle childhood.

Whether and how these more adaptive patterns come into play for young blind children in the course of development, and why this experience is less common for autistic children, who despite growth and progress in response to intervention, continue to present with serious deficits in symbolic understanding and social communicative competence, raises interesting questions about the contributions of environmental experience and the limits of behavioural organization in the developing child (Kopp and Recchia, 1990; Volkmar *et al.*, 1990). Individual differences abound within both populations of children. Whether a young child is able to learn and use behaviours effectively depends on a number of factors, including which system is impaired, the caregiver's ability to provide adequate experience, and the child's ability to integrate the information (Kopp and Recchia, 1990).

Despite differences between the two populations, identifying areas common to the early experience of blind and autistic children which lead to deficits or delays in the development of intersubjectivity can inform our understanding of both populations, and lead to improved strategies for intervention. Clearly, there are many similarities in clinical descriptions of the interactive behaviours of blind and autistic infants. Lack of eye contact, for example, may have a similar impact on the level of contingent responsiveness from caregivers. Children's general lack of ability to attract others' attention may result in less intersubjective experience. Similar deficits in the use of early communicative gestures may contribute to the development of idiosyncratic gestures, language rituals, and a different pace and quality of language development in general, all of which are common to both populations of children (Mulford, 1983; Lord, 1993).

Children must be able to make sense of the environment prior to having meaningful interaction with it (Lewis, 1987). For young blind and autistic children, this making sense, particularly in relation to social-cognitive understanding and intersubjective experience, appears to take extra time and to be highly dependent on adaptive environmental responses (Fraiberg, 1977; Recchia, 1986, 1987, in press; Moore and McConachie, 1995). Intersubjectivity requires the basic ability to establish a common point of reference, which relies on a synchronous interpretation of information. Perceptual and cognitive differences seriously affect the establishment of shared understandings between young children and their caregivers for both autistic and congenitally blind populations.

Caregiver contributions to intersubjective experience

The development of a communicative framework of gestures and signals between mothers and their infants has been shown to function as a first step toward recognition and sharing of emotional states, interpreting and anticipating others' reactions, and understanding relationships between people (Dunn, 1988). For both congenitally blind and autistic children, gestures and signals do not always serve the adaptive function of communication. In fact, many autistic children never develop a meaningful communication system (Paul, 1987). Congenitally blind children are often significantly delayed in their use of gestures for communicative purposes; Rowland (1983), for example, observed a complete absence of conventional gestures in three young blind children and their mothers over a six-month period.

In general, findings from studies of early social communication indicate deviant uses of language, such as echolalia, and personal pronoun and deictic term confusion, in both congenitally blind children and in those autistic children who develop language (Rowland, 1983; Kekelis and Andersen, 1984; Paul, 1987). Children often do not respond when they are expected to, and when they do respond, their communication styles may be challenging for caregivers, who are perplexed by idiosyncratic speech patterns and word use. Over time, the level and quality of caregiver responsiveness may be affected by these reduced and deviant cues from children (Lewis, 1987; Moore and McConachie, 1995).

Social interactions require contingent verbal or non-verbal communication patterns, engaged in by both members of an interactive dyad (Kopp and Recchia, 1990). However, when one social partner is an infant with developmental delays or disabilities, the caregiver often must take on a greater share of the responsibility for dyadic interaction. Caregivers' ability to understand how children experience the environment, and to make their language and communication relevant and pertinent to this experience, is crucial to the development of an effective communication system (Lewis, 1987).

Hobson and colleagues' argument (Chapter 9) that early interactive experience is necessary for later symbolic understanding provides a specific model for the importance of early caregiver–child communication, particularly within populations at greatest risk for deviations in social-cognitive development. Social relationships, regardless of disability status, depend on the quality of caregiver–child interactions (Sostek, 1991). Although it is the child, not the parent, who initially presents a developmental deviation in the case of blindness and autism, because intersubjectivity is necessarily an interactive process, it is the task of the dyad to establish points of synchronous understanding. Joint reference in the face of developmental deviance may not proceed automatically, without careful and sensitive caregiver adaptations (Lewis, 1987; Sostek, 1991).

Early relationship factors

Much has been written about both the importance of the early parent–infant relationship and the impact of disability on caregivers (for example, Lamb and Easterbrooks, 1981; Clark and Seifer, 1985), and that literature will not be reviewed here. However, one issue which presents an interesting question regarding some developmentally relevant differences between congenitally blind and autistic infants is the time of diagnosis. Congenitally blind children (those with severe visual impairments which result in no more than minimal light perception) commonly receive a visual diagnosis early in the first year of life. For children with autism, on the other hand, it is not uncommon for a diagnosis to be delayed until well into the second year of life, particularly for children who are higher-functioning (Wing and Attwood, 1987; Hobson, 1993). Thus, the psychological impact of coming to terms with the diagnosis, and the effect on caregiver–child interactions, may be very different.

Although studies often retrieve retrospective data indicating caregivers' earlier suspicions of developmental deviation in their autistic children, many families of autistic children do not suspect a developmental problem in the first year of life. Subgroups of autistic children may reach early sensori-motor developmental milestones according to a fairly typical timetable (Wing and Attwood, 1987). More subtle differences in the young autistic child's behaviour may quietly influence the caregiver's responses but, for the most part, many caregivers do not report concerns about their children until social and language delays become evident during toddlerhood. The somewhat insidious nature of autism in very young children is such that one cannot presume the absence of interactive deficits despite their subtlety. However, for many families, the initial impact of diagnosis takes place when children have already developed beyond the tasks of early infancy.

In contrast, for congenitally blind children, delays in the course of early sensori-motor development become obvious within the first six months of life. Children are challenged by motor milestones which require movement in space, and do not generally establish independent exploratory behaviour without environmental adaptations. Thus, caregivers are often called upon to re-evaluate their own ways of responding to their young infants while, at the same time, coming to terms with the diagnosis of blindness. All of this takes place during the vulnerable, formative stages of the early caregiver–child relationship.

Specific challenges to caregiver–child communication

The social-communicative repertoires of congenitally blind children, and children with autism, have several characteristics in common, and these contribute significantly to potential deficits in intersubjective experience. Perceptual differences between the children and their caregivers in these two populations may create ambiguity for caregivers (and other communicative partners). When children perceive stimuli differently from their caregivers, it is often difficult for caregivers to take their point of view.

Both blind and autistic children often demonstrate a reduced sense of agency in their interactions with environmental stimuli (McGurk, 1983; Lord, 1993), providing caregivers with insufficient feedback to evoke contingent responses. Although their behaviours may be qualitatively different, with autistic children characteristically more detached and blind children more passive, their interactive responses may be equally ineffective. Lord (1993) has noted that, for autistic children, emotional expression is particularly lacking in co-ordination with other social behaviour, and this deficit becomes even more pronounced in unstructured situations.

Low responsiveness in children can also cause caregivers to over-compensate in their level of responding. As a result, social deficits may be masked early on if dyads become accustomed to communicating within a particular structure and routine. When parents take the initiative too often, young autistic and blind children may respond but be less likely to initiate outside of the imposed structure (Lord, 1993). Even when they do respond, these children may need continual prompting for each turn they take (Rowland, 1983). Caregivers themselves can become routinized in their own interactive behaviours with children, inadvertently reinforcing the deficits.

Several researchers have noted deficits in interactive communication between caregivers and their children, including a lack of adaptive responsiveness on the part of adult partners (Rowland, 1983; Kekelis and Andersen, 1984; Lewis, 1987; Moore and McConachie, 1994; 1995). Parents tend to use more labels and questions with both blind and autistic children, rather than responding to their children's initiations. Rowland (1983) found that mothers of blind children rarely imitated their infants' vocalizations, resulting in little encouragement of the infant's own communication patterns. Moore and McConachie (1995) found that parents used more verbal initiations than action-oriented strategies with their pre-verbal blind children. They tended to ask questions even though their children could not answer them, rather than stimulating conversational exchanges. Similar to caregivers of sighted children who are delayed in their language development, these caregivers also talked less about things their children were attending to, and tended to use general rather than specific descriptions of objects (for example, 'nice ball' rather than 'round ball').

Developmental adaptations and expected outcomes

Judging by the numbers of older children with autism and congenital blindness who continue to demonstrate severe deficits in social-cognitive understanding (Fraiberg, 1977; Hobson, 1993), challenges to the development of intersubjectivity do not appear easily resolved. Ongoing communication with their blind or autistic children may continue to be difficult for caregivers, as children's responses reflect further deviations in their perceptual and cognitive processing. Caregivers are challenged by what may appear to be ambiguous signals which do not conform to their expectations. Whether and how caregivers make sense of those signals, and ultimately respond to them, can have serious implications for their children's subsequent developmental adaptations.

The process of developing intersubjectivity in the face of sensory and perceptual impairments is neither adequately described in the liter-ature nor easily measured in research paradigms. However, both care-givers and children often develop creative ways to help each other to gain access to their thinking. Parents and their blind children, for example, do indeed find their own idiosyncratic ways to communicate (Recchia, 1993; 1996), although some dyads discover more adaptive solutions than others. Studies have shown that parents often need help to read and interpret atypical signals.

In order to adequately assess overall intervention needs in the dyad, it is necessary to look at both the child's predisposition toward disability and the adequacy of the psycho-social environment (Provence and Dahl, 1987). Most blind children have the capacity to respond to auditory and tactual stimuli in somewhat predictable ways (providing touch and hearing receptors function normally). But even those children who are neurologically intact in infancy may migrate toward a deviant developmental course without appropriate feedback and stimulation from the caregiving environment. Blind children's ability to access potential alternative pathways to developmental competences may depend on the resilience of their interactive relationships. In fact, some of the factors identified as most predictive of blind children's adjustment to their own disability are the parent's acceptance of the handicap, their awareness of the child's signals and their ability to read them, and their confidence in their role as parents (Lewis, 1987).

The most promising indications for blind children's ability to compensate for early deficits in developing intersubjectivity come with language. As language competence increases, children may be better able to communicate with their caregivers using a shared format (Lewis, 1987). Once young blind children can use language to access their caregivers more effectively, reciprocal communicative interactions are more likely to take place. However, because the foundations of meaningful language are formed well before its onset, failure to sufficiently engage with caregivers in infancy may interfere with children's later linguistic capacity.

Prognoses for appropriate language development are much poorer for autistic children (Paul, 1987). Furthermore, unlike the congenitally blind, in many autistic children the lack of predictable responsiveness spans several sensory modalities (Lord, 1993). The degree to which children's perceptions differ may tax the communicative capacity of the dyad even further. Thus, these two populations, despite similarities in behavioural manifestations, present different kinds of challenges for developmental adaptations and interventions.

Differences in time of diagnosis, as discussed previously, may also contribute to the complexity of the psychosocial environment of the developing young child. Early diagnosis optimizes the growth of early relationships which may rely on intervention for their success. Additionally, when intervention begins early, caregivers are involved in their children's developmental successes, and may have more opportunities to prevent potential problems before they occur.

Early intervention with congenitally blind children is most effective when it is done preventatively (Fraiberg, 1977). Often intervention strategies focus on caregivers, encouraging them as soon as possible to adapt their presentation and communication styles to meet the needs of their children (Recchia, 1986). In this way, interventions help parents to increase their level of awareness of children's ways of accessing the environment; make social connections with their children; and observe their children in ways which allow them to take the child's perspective, rather than simply reacting to their children's responses.

Differences in the aetiology and the developmental course of autism may complicate the process of early intervention. Many autistic children go through periods of developmental regression, which may have a negative psychological impact on their caregivers, creating further challenges to the development of interactive competence and intersubjectivity. However, there is some evidence that those children who are able to develop stronger early connections with caregivers have better long-term outcomes (Volkmar, 1987).

Conclusion

The establishment of early intersubjectivity between caregivers and their young children is considered essential to the development of later child competences, particularly in the areas of social cognition and communication. For children with congenital blindness or autism, who are at considerable risk for developmental delays and deviations in these areas, intersubjectivity takes on a new significance for child–caregiver dyads. Evidence from both populations indicates that establishing positive early social connections between infants and their caregivers may contribute significantly to individual differences in outcomes.

The degree to which early intervention can influence the developmental course of young children with blindness or autism is neither easily predictable nor simply evaluated. Many factors contribute to optimizing the development of competence, not least of which is the caregivers' ability to adapt their responses to accommodate perceptual differences in their children. Even the most effective and sensitive caregivers, however, may be limited in their ability to compensate for serious developmental deviations in their children.

Intersubjective experience may remain elusive, particularly for children with autism, who, for reasons still not completely clear to us, seem unable to truly take the perspective of another, despite cognitive competence and intervention. For the congenitally blind, the prognosis is sometimes improved, particularly when intervention begins early and focuses on optimizing the caregiver–child relationship and developing linguistic competence.

The question remains whether accessing alternative sensory and perceptual pathways truly provides unconventional routes to the same endpoints (Moore and McConachie, 1994). In other words, can experience perceived in such different ways be jointly understood, or does there remain a barrier to sharing the meaning of events? What are the limits to generalizing shared understanding beyond well-established relationships?

The answers to these and other questions may lie in more careful and systematic observations of children with congenital blindness and children with autism, particularly within the context of early relationships with caregivers. We have begun to identify those competences which are lacking in these two populations. Perhaps it is time to examine more thoroughly the processes by which children and their caregivers are attempting to compensate for developmental deviations.

References

Bruner, J. (1977). Early social interaction and language acquisition. In H. R. Schaffer (Ed.), *Studies in Mother–Infant Interaction*. London: Academic Press.

Campos, J. J. and Stenberg, C. (1981). Perception, appraisal and emotion: The onset of social referencing. In M. Lamb and L. Sherrod (Eds), *Infant Social Cognition*. Hillsdale, NJ: Erlbaum.

Clark, G. M. and Seifer, R. (1985). Assessment of parents' interactions with their developmentally delayed infants. *Infant Mental Health Journal, 6*, 214–225.

Dunn, J. (1988). *The Beginnings of Social Understanding*. Cambridge: Harvard University Press.

Fraiberg, S. (1977). *Insights from the Blind*. New York: Basic Books.

Frith, U. and Baron-Cohen, S. (1987). Perception in autistic children. In D. J. Cohen and A. M. Donnellan (Eds), *Handbook of Autism and Pervasive Developmental Disorders*. New York: Wiley.

Hobson, R. P. (1993). *Autism and the Development of Mind*. Hove: Erlbaum.

Hornik, G. N., Risenhoover, N. and Gunnar, M. (1987). Effects of maternal positive, neutral, and negative affective communications on infant responses to new toys. *Child Development, 58*, 937–944.

Kekelis, L. S. and Andersen, E. W. (1984). Family communication styles and language development. *Journal of Visual Impairment and Blindness, 78*, 54–65.

Klinnert, M. D. (1984). The regulation of infant behaviour by maternal facial expression. *Infant Behavior and Development, 7*, 447–465.

Klinnert, M. D., Campos, J. J., Sorce, J. F., Emde, R. N. and Svejda, M. (1983). Emotions as behavior regulators: Social referencing in infancy. In R. Plutchik and H. Kellerman (Eds), *The Emotions: Vol. 2*. New York: Academic Press.

Kopp, C. B. and Recchia, S. L. (1990). The issue of multiple pathways in the development of handicapped children. In R. M. Hodapp, J. A. Burack and E. Zigler (Eds), *Issues in the Developmental Approach to Mental Retardation*. Cambridge: Cambridge University Press.

Lamb, M. E. and Easterbrooks, M. A. (1981). Individual differences in parental sensitivity: origins, components, and consequences. In M. E. Lamb and L. Sherrod (Eds), *Infant Social Cognition*. Hillsdale, NJ: Erlbaum.

Landau, B. (1991). Knowledge and its expression in the blind child. In D. P. Keating and H. Rosen (Eds), *Constructivist Perspectives in Developmental Psychopathology and Atypical Development*. Hillsdale, NJ: Erlbaum.

Lewis, V. (1987). *Development and Handicap*. Oxford: Basil Blackwell.

Lord, C. (1993). Early social development in autism. In E. Schopler, M. E. Van Bourgondie and M. M. Bristol (Eds), *Preschool Issues in Autism*. New York: Plenum.

McGurk, H. (1983). Effectance motivation. In A. E. Mills (Ed.), *Language Acquisition in the Blind Child: Normal and deficient*. Kent: Croom Helm.

Moore, V. and McConachie, H. (1994). Communication between blind and severely visually impaired children and their parents. *British Journal of Developmental Psychology, 12*, 491–502.

Moore, V. and McConachie, H. (1995). How parents can help young visually-impaired children to communicate. *Health Visitor, 68*, 105–107.

Mulford, R. (1983). Referential development in blind children. In A. E. Mills (Ed.), *Language Acquisition in the Blind Child: Normal and deficient*. Kent: Croom Helm.

Paul, R. (1987). Communication. In D. J. Cohen and A. M. Donnellan (Eds), *Handbook of Autism and Pervasive Developmental Disorders*. New York: Wiley.

Provence, S. and Dahl, E. K. (1987). Disorders of atypical development: Diagnostic issues raised by a spectrum disorder. In D. J. Cohen and A. M. Donnellan (Eds), *Handbook of Autism and Pervasive Developmental Disorders*. New York: Wiley.

Recchia, S. L. (1986). *Welcome to the World: Toys and activities for the visually impaired infant*. (Available from Blind Children's Center, 4120 Marathon St., P. O. Box 29159, Los Angeles, California 90029.)

Recchia, S. L. (1987). *Learning to Play: Common concerns for the visually impaired preschool child*. Los Angeles: Blind Children's Center (ERIC document reproduction service number ED 292240).

Recchia, S. L. (1993). How visually impaired toddlers and their mothers respond to ambiguous stimuli. Unpublished doctoral dissertation, University of California, Los Angeles.

Recchia, S. L. (1996). Parent–child communication and response to ambiguous stimuli: A multiple case study analysis of young children with severe visual impairments and their families. Unpublished manuscript, Teachers College, Columbia University.

Recchia, S. L. (in press). Play and concept development in infants with severe visual impairments: A constructivist view. *Journal of Visual Impairment and Blindness*.

Rogers, S. J. and Newhart-Larson, S. (1989). Characteristics of infantile autism in five children with Leber's congenital amaurosis. *Developmental Medicine and Child Neurology, 31*, 598–608.

Rowland, C. (1983). Patterns of interaction between three blind infants and their mothers. In A. E. Mills (Ed.), *Language Acquisition in the Blind Child: Normal and deficient*. Kent: Croom Helm.

Sigman, M., Mundy, P., Sherman, T. and Ungerer, J. (1986). Social interactions of autistic, mentally retarded, and normal children and their caregivers. *Journal of Child Psychology and Psychiatry, 27*, 647–656.

Sigman, M., Ungerer, J. A., Mundy, P. and Sherman, T. (1987). Cognition in autistic children. In D. J. Cohen and A. M. Donnellan (Eds), *Handbook of Autism and Pervasive Developmental Disorders*. New York: Wiley.

Sostek, A. (1991). Development of the blind child: Implications for assessment and intervention. In D. P. Keating and H. Rosen (Eds), *Constructivist*

Perspectives in Developmental Psychopathology and Atypical Development. Hillsdale, N. J.: Erlbaum.

Stern, D. (1985). *The Interpersonal World of the Infant.* New York: Basic Books.

Volkmar, F. R. (1987). Social Development. In D. J. Cohen and A. M. Donnellan (Eds), *Handbook of Autism and Pervasive Developmental Disorders.* New York: Wiley.

Volkmar, F. R., Burack, J. A. and Cohen, D. J. (1990). Deviance and developmental approaches in the study of autism. In R. M. Hodapp, J. A. Burack, and E. Zigler (Eds), *Issues in the Developmental Approach to Mental Retardation.* New York: Cambridge University Press.

Warren, D. H. (1984). *Blindness and Early Childhood Development.* New York: American Foundation for the Blind.

Warren, D. H. (1994). *Blindness and Children: An individual differences approach.* Cambridge: Cambridge University Press.

Wing, L. and Attwood, A. J. (1987). Syndromes of autism and atypical development. In D. J. Cohen and A. M. Donnellan (Eds), *Handbook of Autism and Pervasive Developmental Disorders.* New York: Wiley.

Chapter Ten

Reflections on blind children and developmental psychology

Glyn M. Collis and Vicky Lewis

A number of important general issues were raised in Chapter 1. In particular, we asked how we should seek to comprehend, in comparable terms, the psychological development of both sighted children and blind children; how we should structure our research endeavours so that advances in our understanding of development in one case can most enhance our understanding in the other; and how we should proceed so as to avoid the twin dangers of adopting a negative stance toward atypical development in comparison to typical development, and the playing down of *individual* differences in our search for consistent *inter-group* differences.

One conclusion is immediately obvious from the chapters of this book. Theoretical and empirical advances in the study of normal development are very important in guiding the way we think about development in blind children and children with other disabilities. Take, for instance, Preisler's use of Stern's (1985) description of the main trends in social development (Chapter 6). Without some such theoretical framework, sensitively used, the account of the development of the children in her study would have been severely impoverished. Stern's framework may not be the only one that could serve this purpose, but there are not many alternatives which are so well-founded on a combination of sensitive observation of individual children and their parents as unique dyads, systematic quantitative analyses of the processes of early social interactions across a number of dyads, and interpretation of the findings in ways that are both original and clearly linked to contemporary understanding of the cognitive and emotional lives of young children and their parents.

Millar and Harris and Barlow-Brown's discussions of the work on braille reading are similarly informed by concepts used in research on how sighted people read print, and take an imaginative but also cautious outlook on both the similarities and differences between braille reading and print reading. For example, Harris and Barlow-Brown highlight the implications of young blind children not having the kind of incidental exposure to print that contributes to sighted children's early knowledge about the written alphabet. Less self-evident is the point, arising from Barlow-Brown's work, that blind children may have access to word-level knowledge as well as letter-level knowledge, even at the earliest stages of learning to read braille. Both these points arise from considering together, and with sensitivity, what is known about print reading and what is known about blindness and braille reading.

In both these domains of social development and reading development, the interplay between our framework for understanding normal development, and our observations of the similarities to, and differences from, atypical development, seem to have the most scope for informing practice. Stern's account of early social development, like Bowlby's before him, emphasizes the role of emerging representations of self, of other individuals, and of self–other relationships. These representations are believed to be built on the experience of interacting with others; in turn, they provide a working knowledge base which guides initiation and participation in social encounters, the conduct of future interactions, the interpretation of further social experience, and the emergence of new social relationships. Moreover, representations are believed to be the vehicle of longer-term developmental consequences of experience, and the key to understanding both persistence and change of individual characteristics over time (Bretherton, 1987). As Preisler shows, this framework provides a useful backdrop for research on how differences between sighted and blind children in the characteristics of their social *interactions* might influence the characteristics of their social *representations*. However, a great deal remains to be learned about how and why some features of social experience play a major role in shaping representations and others do not. When we understand more about the impact of blindness on social representations, we will have additional answers to these 'How?' and 'Why?' questions that will apply to sighted children as well.

Preisler describes how some, but not all, of the parents of her blind children gave running commentaries about what their child was doing, their own feelings toward the child and so on. It is plausible that this linguistic input could be an alternative source of information that helps structure the children's representations. However, it is not uncommon for parents of sighted children also to give running commentaries about their sighted children's behaviour. Early work on this topic focused on mothers naming objects that the children were looking at, but that is just one aspect of the talk which often accompanies parental monitoring of children's ongoing activities (Collis, 1977). As Preisler points out, a good case can be made that verbal input about shared

131

feelings makes an important contribution to the development of representations of self, others and relationships (Dunn, 1994). Thus, rather than blind and sighted children building social representations in different ways, it seems more like a different balance between various possibilities – exactly what we would expect from a view that the processes of development are resilient and flexible, with a fair amount of scope for compensation and multiple pathways, as emphasized by Locke in Chapter 3.

Nonetheless, Preisler's outlook has a note of pessimism, but this is less to do with events intrinsic to the children, and more to do with their social partners – parents and teachers. Preisler's blind children seemed to do the right things to provoke social interaction, at least in the early stages, but the responses of others were not sufficiently adapted to the children's needs. This sort of process is thought to underlie, for example, the tendency for parents of blind children to be rather directive when speaking to their children. The flexibility and resilience of the developmental process thus seems more limited when we consider causal routes external to the mind of the child, particularly the expectations, beliefs and response styles of adults. This kind of process is well known in studies of social influences on the development of other groups of children with disabilities. For example, the literature on language learning in deaf children repeatedly alludes to the difficulties that hearing adults have in attuning themselves to the particular needs of young deaf children in social interaction (for example, Wood, Wood, Griffiths and Howarth, 1986). What is less clear is whether the same style of parental behaviour would affect children who do not have an intrinsic disadvantage such as a lack of vision or hearing.

Preisler's discussion is wide-ranging, taking in the full range of developmental changes and challenges faced by blind children as they grow up. Recchia's focus (Chapter 9) is much narrower, concentrating on the development of intersubjectivity in the early years, but she makes very similar points about the role of parents and carers in the development of this domain of psychological functioning, and the implications for intervention. Although at first sight it might seem fairly straightforward to devise intervention programmes to train parents and teachers in appropriate modes of responding, this has proven to be far from straightforward and not particularly successful. The precise reasons for this remain poorly understood, but it seems useful to formulate the problem as a mismatch between the representational systems of parent and child. An important question for the future is how their working models of each other and of their relationship can be changed so as to reduce the mismatch. There are interesting analogies to be drawn with work on teachers' interactions with deaf children and the improvements that can be brought about by changing the teachers' perceptions of the goals of conversing with children, and their own role in these conversations (Wood et al., 1986).

Landau's discussion (Chapter 2) of language development in blind children is generally optimistic. Her work maintains contact with the view that research should inform practice as it applies to blind children, and in addition it illustrates particularly clearly how studying development in blind children can give us insights into the processes of development in sighted children. Starting from findings that blind children do not seem to have particular problems with syntax, and the implausibility of the position that syntax could be acquired independently of meaning, Landau illustrates how some of the more obvious assumptions about how young (sighted) children learn mappings between language and meaning are too simple to explain language acquisition in blind children, and most likely are not an adequate account for sighted children either. The evidence from blind children is very persuasive about the significance of syntactic information in the acquisition of word meaning in sighted as well as in blind children. While it is true that a role for syntax had been established for some time (Katz, Baker and MacNamara, 1974), the work with blind children was a major impetus for the development and refinement of the syntactic bootstrapping models of language development in both sighted and blind children (Landau and Gleitman, 1985; Gleitman, 1990). The importance of this work for theoretical models of language acquisition is clear even if one does not adhere to the strong assumptions of innate syntactic knowledge favoured by Gleitman.

Landau's work on blind children's concepts of objects and their acquisition of language (see also Landau, 1991) constitutes a significant challenge to the widely-held assumption that vision has a special significance for cognitive functioning and therefore that psychological development in children who are blind from birth should be radically different from sighted children. Fogel (Chapter 7) also addresses this fundamental issue. He is comfortable with the view that the absence of vision does not dramatically reduce the capabilities of a cognitive system. However, he argues that a cognitive system which grows in the context of readily available visual information really is subtly different from cognition growing in the absence of vision. This is primarily because vision is a simultaneous and continuous sensory system, whereas the other major senses – touch and audition – are sequential. Vision gives (relatively) immediate access to information on parts and wholes, whereas touch and audition need a narrative type of cognition to extract holistic meaning. Thus cognitive schemas derived primarily from a narrative analysis of sequential information in touch and hearing will be different from schemas derived from immediate part-whole processing. Fogel speculates that narrative analysis brings about a bias in the system in favour of deliberate rather than spontaneous action.

Perhaps this shows the dangers of single case approaches, for Fogel's own experiences, plus those reported by Truitt (1982), are not a strong database on which to rest conclusions. But it does provide a platform for further empirical study. Fogel draws a parallel with the distinction between the narrative and paradigmatic ways of knowing (Bruner, 1986) arising from research on the development of cognition in non-disabled people. The hypothesis that Fogel articulates for the impact of lack of visual impairment on style of cognitive processing thus provides a testbed for the generality of the principle that there are two ways of knowing.

Hobson *et al.* (Chapter 8) focus on a hypothesis that vision has a special role in one particular developmental process. They examine the implications of this hypothesis for children with autism as well as children who are blind and those who are sighted and developing typically. The hypothesis is that, in the normal course of development, vision has an important role in the child becoming aware that others can adopt a psychological stance towards a particular object that is different from the child's own stance toward the same object. This growing awareness is an important part of a package of cognitive advances. The package includes the disembedding of the infant's thoughts from the here and now, the emergence of reflective thought, the tacit understanding that thoughts as symbols are different from things and that others have attitudes towards objects and events. Moreover, not only do some blind children exhibit problems in this domain of early cognition, so too do children with autism, although their difficulties most likely arise from problems in interpreting what they see rather than a lack of seeing. As Hobson and his colleagues make absolutely clear, this is a hypothesis rather than a conclusion. But it is a hypothesis derived from observations of sighted children with autism and sighted children who are developing normally (Hobson, 1993) as well as children who are severely visually impaired. We hope this hypothesis, and others like it (for example, Rogers and Pennington, 1991) will provoke the kind of empirical investigation that will take us nearer an integrative theory of development, encompassing the developmental characteristics of children with and without disabilities.

What has been achieved and what remains to be done?

The contributions to this book clearly show that the most productive work on blind children is done when researchers succeed in trying to glimpse the world as it is perceived by a blind child, rather than proceeding by uncritically assuming that what sighted people apprehend through vision points to inevitable gaps in the way that blind children comprehend the world. Landau's work on blind children's understanding of objects (Landau, 1993) very clearly illustrates the importance of trying to take the child's point of view.

While bland empirical comparisons between blind and sighted children are likely to be singularly unproductive, the work represented in this volume clearly shows that the best research is likely to be informed by theoretical insights into developmental processes in typically developing sighted children. In turn, insights from the development of blind children will influence developmental theory as a whole. Indeed, the prospect looks bright for theoretical accounts of development which can genuinely account for developmental processes in children with various types of disability and in children who have no disability.

It is clear that research can be extremely successful even though it is seldom possible to work with more than small numbers of children. There is a willingness to learn as much as possible from single case studies (for example, Fraiberg, 1977; Pring, 1992) and from autobiographical accounts such as Fogel's, but this is matched with an understanding that conclusions need to be tested for their generality across a number of individuals and integrated with theory. Preisler's qualitative longitudinal study of a cohort of children illustrates one strategy for developing the case study approach. Another strategy is well illustrated by the work of Hobson and his colleagues who sought to make sense of clinical descriptions by Fraiberg and others. They drew on insights from work on children with autism, and used data from both blind and sighted children to test their ideas.

All the research described in this volume has clear relevance for practice, not because it points to immediate solutions or off-the-shelf interventions, but because it advances our understanding of what is happening to blind children, and sometimes what is failing to happen, at the level of process. The work on interaction and communication points to the need for adults to see social processes from the child's point of view, and especially the manner in which play and social interaction go together. If blind children are to be integrated with sighted children, then ways have to be found to break down the barriers preventing cross-group symbolic play, as described by Preisler, and 'managing' free play so that blind children can join in. The scope for exploiting the sharing of word games between blind and sighted children which Preisler reports working quite well, needs to be explored. Fogel's point that apparent oddness can indicate precocity in certain skills rather than deficiency, deserves more exposure that it gets at present and needs to be at the forefront of every practitioner's mind.

An issue which has not been adequately dealt with in this book is the problem of multiple handicap. This issue is probably the most significant challenge for practice, theory, and for empirical research as we approach the 21st century. It is significant for practice because of the numbers of children involved relative to the numbers with blindness but no other significant impairment. It is significant for theory because it is not clear what kind of models might be appropriate. It is significant for empirical work because of the diversity among the children

involved, and because of the uncertainty as to precisely what functional systems are damaged – the more 'multiple' the damage, the harder
it is to identify the components of damage. It does not seem much of an
empirical advance simply to be able to obtain a 'how much' aggregate
measure of disability. However, we are broadly optimistic. The last 20
years or so have seen a steady consolidation of developmental theory
so that it covers the development of children with and without disabilities, usually at the level of domain-specific insights or specific issues in
development rather than as a Grand Developmental Theory in the
Piagetian vein. It does not seem too much to expect that we will soon
see theory driving research into the problem of multiple handicap.

References

Bretherton, I. (1987). New perspectives on attachment relations: security, communication and internal working models. In. J. D. Osofsky (Ed.), *Handbook of
Infant Development, 2nd edn.* New York: Wiley.

Bruner, J. (1986). *Actual Minds, Possible Worlds.* Cambridge, MA: Harvard
University Press.

Collis, G. M. (1977). Visual co-orientation and maternal speech. In H. R.
Schaffer (Ed.), *Studies in Mother–Infant Interaction.* London: Academic Press.

Dunn, J. (1994). Changing minds and changing relationships. In C. Lewis and
P. Mitchell (Eds), *Children's Early Understanding of Mind.* Hove: Erlbaum.

Fraiberg, S. (1977). *Insights from the Blind.* New York: Basic Books.

Gleitman, L. R. (1990). The structural sources of verb meanings. *Language
Acquisition, 1,* 3–55.

Hobson, R. P. (1993). *Autism and the Development of Mind.* Hove: Erlbaum.

Katz, N., Baker, E. and MacNamara, J. (1974). What's in a name? A study of
how children learn common and proper names. *Child Development, 45,*
469–473.

Landau, B. (1991). Knowledge and its expression in the blind child. In D. P.
Keating and H. Rosen (Eds), *Constructivist Perspectives on Developmental
Psychopathology and Atypical Development.* Hillsdale, NJ: Erlbaum.

Landau, B. and Gleitman, L. R. (1985). *Language and Experience: Evidence from the
blind child.* Cambridge, MA: Harvard University Press.

Pring, L. (1992). More than meets the eye. In R. Campbell (Ed.), *Mental Lives:
Case studies in cognition.* Oxford: Blackwell.

Rogers, S. J. and Pennington, B. F. (1991). A theoretical approach to the deficits
of infantile autism. *Development and Psychopathology, 3,* 137–162.

Stern, D. (1985). *The Interpersonal World of the Infant.* New York: Basic Books.

Truitt, A. (1982). *Daybook: The journal of an artist.* New York: Penguin.

Wood, D., Wood, H., Griffiths, A. and Howarth, I. (1986). *Teaching and Talking
with Deaf Children.* Chichester: Wiley.

Author Index

Bold italicized page numbers indicate where the full reference to the author's work may be found

Subject Index